SADLIER'S
Coming to Faith Program

COMING TO
GOD

Dr. Gerard F. Baumbach

Dr. Eleanor Ann Brownell

Moya Gullage

Helen Hemmer, I. H. M.

Gloria Hutchinson

Dr. Norman F. Josaitis

Rev. Michael J. Lanning, O. F. M.

Dr. Marie Murphy

Karen Ryan

Joseph F. Sweeney

Patricia Andrews

> The Ad Hoc Committee
> to Oversee the Use of the Catechism,
> National Conference of Catholic Bishops,
> has found this catechetical text to be
> in conformity with the
> *Catechism of the Catholic Church.*

with

Dr. Thomas H. Groome
Boston College

Official Theological Consultant
   The Most Rev. Edward K. Braxton, Ph. D., S. T. D.

Scriptural Consultant
   Rev. Donald Senior, C. P., Ph. D., S. T. D.

Catechetical and Liturgical Consultants
   Dr. Gerard F. Baumbach
   Dr. Eleanor Ann Brownell

Pastoral Consultants
   Rev. Msgr. John F. Barry
   Rev. Virgilio P. Elizondo, Ph.D., S. T. D.

William H. Sadlier, Inc.
9 Pine Street
New York, New York 10005-1002
http://www.sadlier.com

CONTENTS

Unit 3   Jesus Christ Gives Us the Church   page

Doctrine: Catholic Teaching   **Faith Alive at Home and in the Parish**

Unit 4	Our Catholic Church and Us	page

Doctrine: Catholic Teaching

Faith Alive at Home and in the Parish

DEAR GIRLS AND BOYS,

Coming to God is your book. It has been written especially for you. Your religion book will help you to come to know and love God more and more.

In your **Coming to God** book you will find wonderful things to think about, to talk about, to do and to learn by heart. You will find:

- stories about boys and girls who love God just as you do;
- prayers to help you listen and talk to God;
- stories from the Bible, especially about Jesus, God's own Son;
- the story of our Catholic Church;
- action prayers to help you celebrate God's love for you and all people.

All of these things can help you to grow in your love for God and other people. We hope you will have a wonderful time this year as you come closer to God. During the year be sure to share what you learn and think and feel with your family.

All of Us in the Sadlier Family

Here We Are, God!

God, help us
to learn about
You together.

Our Life

Let's take turns. Tell everyone your name.
Share your own special hello with us.

Sharing Life

Sing this coming together song.
(To the tune of "Did You Ever See?")

♫ Oh, we all have come together
Together, together.
Oh, we all have come together
To learn about God.

We're happy to be here.
We'll all help each other.
Oh, we all have come together
To learn about God. ♫

How do you feel to be learning about God?

God wants us to learn
many things this year.
We will learn many wonderful
things about God together.

We can help one another
listen and learn about God's love.

We can share our Catholic faith
as we read and listen to stories
from the Bible.

We can share our faith by drawing,
singing, and praying together.

We can help one
another to live
our faith.

COMING TO FAITH

Look at your *Coming to God* book.
Is there something you want
to learn about God this year?
Take turns telling a friend about it.

PRACTICING FAITH

Put your hands flat on the floor.
Pray,
† God, we know that You are with us.

Join hands with your friends
beside you.
Pray,
† God, help us to learn together
   many wonderful things about You.

Hold your right hand over your heart.
Pray,
† God, help us to listen and learn
about Your wonderful love.

10

Take a few minutes to go over the
"Faith Alive" pages with the children.
Encourage them to share the family
prayer at home and to pray these
words with their families at a special
time each day.

FAITH ALIVE

AT HOME AND IN THE PARISH

In this opening lesson your child was welcomed to first grade, both as an individual and as a member of a group. It is important that children feel part of a Christian community, especially your parish community, as they begin to explore together what it means to belong to the family of God.

This year your child's program in learning about our Catholic faith is called *Coming to God*. You have already spent time preparing your child for this continuing growth of coming to God, even without thinking about it. You have, informally and gently, been teaching your child about God and about God's love all along. It will be important that you continue to take an even more active role in guiding your child's growth in faith. Here are some ways the *Coming to God* program might assist you.

■ Talk about each lesson together, including the pictures and artwork, if possible, since they are an essential part of the program. Encourage a conversation about the *Faith Summary* statements. The symbol reminds you to help your child learn these by heart. You might ask a question for each statement.

■ Invite your child to share with you any songs, poems, or experiences of prayer that have been learned or shared. Even before truths of our Catholic faith are fully understood, they can be absorbed through a favorite song or prayer.

■ Use the *Faith Alive at Home and in the Parish* pages (this is the first of them) to continue and to expand your child's catechesis through the experience of the community of faith in your family and in the parish family. There will be a variety of activities on these pages. Try to do at least one with your child.

Family Scripture Moment is offered as a unique opportunity for the family to share faith by "breaking open" God's word together. The "moment" can be as brief or as long as you wish. A simple outline is suggested as one way to use this time together.

■ **Gather** together as a family. All can participate from the youngest to the oldest.

■ **Listen** to God's word as it is read, slowly and expressively, by a family member.

■ **Share** what you hear from the reading that touches your own life. Give time for each one to do this.

■ **Consider** the points suggested as a way to come to a deeper understanding of God's word.

■ **Reflect** on and share any new understandings.

■ **Decide** as a family how you will try to live God's word.

In this first grade text, some lines from the beautiful Gospel of Luke will be suggested for family faith sharing, prayer, and reflection.

Learn by heart Faith Summary

- We help one another learn about God's love.
- We share our Catholic faith.

A Family Prayer
Pray this prayer
with your family.

†Dear God, help us this year to come closer to You. Amen.

When you and your child have worked together on the *Faith Summary* and any of these family activities, invite your child to choose a sticker and place it at the top of the *Faith Alive* page. Do this for every *Faith Alive* page that follows.

Make a Faith Alive Keeper

You need a sheet of cardboard or heavy paper, larger and twice as wide as this page. Fold it in half. Then fold the bottom ends in about 3 inches to make flaps. Tape the flaps. Put your *Faith Alive* pages in your Keeper.

Family Suggestion: You may wish to provide your child with a variety of stickers that can be used on the review page throughout the year.

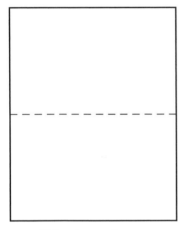

1 Take sheet of paper

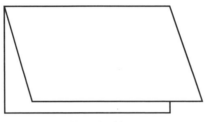

2 Fold in half

3 Fold over sides

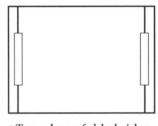

4 Tape down folded sides

5 Write "Faith Alive Keeper" on front

FAMILY SCRIPTURE MOMENT

Gather and **Listen** as the very first words of Luke's Gospel are read expressively.

Dear Theophilus: Many people have done their best to write a report of the things that have taken place among us [concerning Jesus of Nazareth]. They wrote what we have been told by those who saw these things from the beginning and who proclaimed the message. Because I have carefully studied all these matters from their beginning, I thought it would be good to write an orderly account for you. I do this so that you will know the full truth about everything which you have been taught.

From Luke 1:1–4

Share What is Luke saying to us here?

Consider for family enrichment:

■ Luke's Gospel is addressed to Theophilus ("friend or lover of God") and to us. It assures us that God's promises have been fulfilled in Jesus.

■ Luke assures his readers that his message is true and is based on eyewitness accounts. He invites us to deepen our faith in Jesus.

Reflect and **Decide** After rereading Luke 1:1–4, share your hopes in exploring Luke's Gospel together. Pray for hearts and minds open to the good news of Jesus.

1 God Made the World

Our Life

Do you like to discover things in the world?
Imagine you are outside in your favorite place.

Look up.
What do you discover?

Look all around.
What do you discover?

Look down.
What do you discover?

Name some more of your favorite things in our world.

Sharing Life

Why is our world so wonderful?

Do you know who made it?

13

God Made the World

Everything good comes
from God our Father.

This is the story of creation
from the Bible.

Read to me from the Bible

God made the sun, the moon,
and the stars.
The light helps us to see.
The light makes us warm.
God said, "It is good."
From Genesis 1:3–4

God made the water and the earth.
He made the plants, trees, and flowers.
God said, "It is good."
From Genesis 1:10–13

God made all living things in our world.
He made all the animals, big and small.
God said, "It is good."
From Genesis 1:24–25

Creation is everything made by God.
All of creation is the Father's gift to us.

All God's creation is good!
We can know God through the things
our heavenly Father made for us.

Coming To Faith

Sing this song about God's
wonderful world.
(To the tune of "The Farmer in the Dell")

♫ The birds fly in the sky.
The fish live in the sea.
We all live in a wonderful world
God made for you and me. ♫

Can you tell or act out how you
feel about God's wonderful world?

Practicing Faith

Finish this prayer with a picture.
I thank You, God, for _____

Take turns praying your picture
prayers.
Then pray together,
† Thank You, God, for all creation.

16

Take a few minutes to go over the
"Faith Alive" pages with the children.
Encourage them to color their thank
you prayer and tell someone in their
family why God's world is wonderful.

FAITH ALIVE AT HOME AND IN THE PARISH

In this lesson your child was reminded that God created the world. When was the last time you and your family took time to feel the wonder and beauty of God's creation in a sunrise or sunset, in a walk through a park, in a rainbow, or in the trusting grasp of your child's hand?

You might ask yourself:

■ *When am I most likely to appreciate God's creation? least likely?*

■ *What will I do this week to help my family experience the wonder of God's creation?*

Talk to your child about the beauty of God's world. Then complete these activities together.

Learn by heart **Faith Summary**

- God the Father made everything.
- All God's creation is good.

Make a Mobile

Trace the moon and as many stars as you want.

Color them yellow. Cut them out. Punch a hole in each one.

Tie them to a clothes hanger with string of different lengths.

Hang your mobile where the air will make it move. It will remind you to thank God for the moon and the stars.

Review

First go over the *Faith Summary* with your child. Then have him or her complete the *Review*. The answers for questions 1–4 appear on page 200. The response to number 5 will help you and your child think about how much she or he has grown to appreciate God's creation. Invite your child to place a sticker on this page.

sticker

Circle the correct answer.

1. God the Father made everything good.   Yes   No

2. God's world is ugly.   Yes   No

3. People made the animals.   Yes   No

4. Creation is everything made by God.   Yes   No

5. How will I thank God for all creation?

_____

_____

FAMILY SCRIPTURE MOMENT

As you **Gather** ask your family what each one thinks is the most important thing in life. Now **Listen:**

Look how the wild flowers grow: they don't work or make clothes for themselves. But I tell you that not even King Solomon with all his wealth had clothes as beautiful as one of these flowers. It is God who clothes the wild grass—grass that is here today and gone tomorrow, burned up in the oven. Won't God be all the more sure to clothe you? What little faith you have!

From Luke 12:27–28

Share What is Jesus trying to teach us here?

Consider for family enrichment:

■ Luke's Gospel contains many of Jesus' sayings and parables about being dependent on God for our happiness rather than on material things.

■ Jesus teaches that we can put our trust in God because God cares for all of creation, but especially for us.

Reflect and **Decide** How do these words of Jesus challenge me to grow in my faith now? What will we do this week as a family to show that we place our trust in God?

18

3   God Gives Us Life

Our Life

What would it be like
if nothing made sounds?

What sounds do lions make?
Can you make these sounds? Do it.

How would you feel
if nothing could move?

How do dolphins move?
Can you move like them? Do it.

Sharing Life

What can a flower do
that a rock cannot do?

What can a lion do
that a flower cannot do?

What can you do that a flower
and a lion cannot do? Why?

God Gives Us Life

All life is a gift from God.
He gives plants, animals, and
all living things the gift of life.

Of all the things God made,
people are the most precious.
People have human life.
Human life is a gift from God.

God said,
"People are very good."
From Genesis 1:27–31

Human life is very precious to God
who gives us the gift of human life
through our parents.

God wants us to care for all
human life as others care for us.

Grace is God's own life and love in us.

God's Own Life

Grace is a special gift we have from God. It is His own life and love in us.

You have God's grace. You can say, "God is my loving Father. I am His own child."

27

COMING TO FAITH

What do you want to say to God about the gift of life?

Celebrate God's gifts of life and grace in you.
Join your friends in a circle.
Make up actions to go with the song.
(To the tune of "Are You Sleeping?")

♫ Who has God's life?
We have God's life.
Yes we do! Yes we do!
Thank You, God, for Your life.
Thank You, God, for Your grace.
We love You. We love You. ♫

PRACTICING FAITH

Life is very precious.
What will you do today
to take care of
the gift of life?

✝ Let us pray together,
Thank you, God, for giving
us Your gifts of life and love.

Take a few minutes to discuss with the children what they and their families might do on the "Faith Alive" pages. After they do the flower activity, they might want to trace it and cut it out at home as a reminder that each one is "God's child."

28

FAITH ALIVE AT HOME AND IN THE PARISH

Life itself is God's first gift to us, a gift that unfolds day by day as we journey in faith as a family. Life is also a call from God to seek the peace of Christ that comes from working for God's reign, or kingdom.

God shares divine life and love with us as the gift of grace. Grace enables us to say, "I am a child of God."

You might ask yourself:

■ *Who or what in our lives and in our society keeps my family and myself from responding fully to God's life?*

■ *What can I do this week to help my child respond each day to God's life in us?*

Have your child complete the activity below. Then talk about how wonderful it is to be a child of God.

Thank God for Life

Talk about your child's birth or adoption. Share how wonderful it is for your family to watch your child grow.

You might want to pray this prayer together.

† Thank You, God, for the gift of (*child's name*).

Faith Summary
Learn by heart

- God gives us the gift of human life.
- Grace is God's own life and love in us.

Paste a picture of yourself in the flower to show you are God's child.

Review

First go over the *Faith Summary* with your child. Then have him or her complete the *Review.* The answers for questions 1–4 appear on page 200. The response to number 5 will help to indicate

whether your child realizes that happiness comes from living as God's child. Invite your child to place a sticker on this page.

sticker

Circle the correct answer.

1. Human life is precious to God.　　Yes　　No

2. Grace is God's life and love in us.　　Yes　　No

3. A flower can hop.　　Yes　　No

4. I have the gift of human life.　　Yes　　No

5. Why am I happy to be God's child?

_____

_____

_____

FAMILY SCRIPTURE MOMENT

Gather and **Listen** to God's word.

When Joseph and Mary had finished doing all that was required by the law of the Lord, they returned to their hometown of Nazareth in Galilee. The child Jesus grew and became strong; He was full of wisdom, and God's blessings were upon Him.

From Luke 2:39–40

Share How have we as individuals grown in wisdom during the past year?

Consider for family enrichment:

■ This reading follows the presentation of Jesus in the Temple by Mary and Joseph. The Law of Moses required Jewish parents to dedicate their firstborn son to God. Mary and Joseph were faithful Jews.

■ We, too, are dedicated to God at Baptism, which makes us children of God. We can grow in wisdom when we work for the reign of God.

Reflect Invite each person to name one way in which he or she hopes to grow in wisdom this week.

Decide Make a family commitment to grow in wisdom together by doing your best to be faithful to these family Scripture moments. Try to get everyone to agree.

30

4   God Knows and Loves Us

Our Life

Let's get to know our friends better.
Talk with a partner about some
favorite things,
    a favorite toy,
    a favorite thing to do outside,
    a favorite thing to do on a rainy day.
Listen carefully to one another.

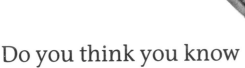

Do you think you know
each other better now?

Sharing Life

How does knowing people
help us love them better?

Do you think God wants us to love
one another? Why?

OUR CATHOLIC FAITH

God Knows and Loves Us

God knows and loves us.
God made us out of love.
God gives us a share in His own life.
We are called God's children.

From 1 John 3:1

God always loves and cares for us.
God's love for us will never end.
He wants us to love one another.

There is only one God.
There are three Persons
in one God,
God the Father,
God the Son,
and God the Holy Spirit.

In the name
of the Father,

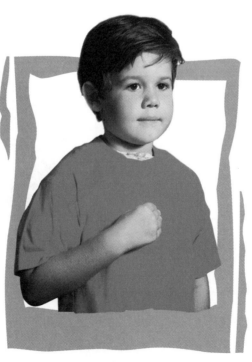

and of the Son,

and of the Holy

We call the three Persons
in one God the Blessed Trinity.

The Sign of the Cross

When we begin our prayers to God,
we say,
† In the name of the Father,
and of the Son,
and of the Holy Spirit. Amen.

We call this the Sign of the Cross.

This prayer can always remind us
of God's great love for us.

Spirit.

Amen.

33

COMING TO FAITH

To show that you are God's child, whisper your name where you see the heart.

God made ♥ and others out of love.

God always loves and cares for ♥ and others.

God wants ♥ and others to love one another.

God loves you so much. How does this make you feel?

PRACTICING FAITH

Think of some people in your parish who show you that God loves you. How will you thank them?

Let us make the sign of the cross together as our closing prayer.

Talk to the children about ways they and their families might use the "Faith Alive" activities. Encourage them to show someone at home how they can make the sign of the cross.

FAITH ALIVE AT HOME AND IN THE PARISH

This week your child learned that God the Father, God the Son, and God the Holy Spirit are each equally and eternally God. Yet our faith is always in one God, a unity of three in one. Our faith in the Blessed Trinity helps us to know, love, and care for one another as God knows, loves, and cares for us.

You might ask yourself:

■ *How does my conviction that God loves me enrich my faith? my family life?*

■ *What will I do to help my family express God's knowing, loving, and caring this week?*

Talk About Caring

Have your child show you pictures of people caring for one another. Ask how each is caring for someone. Mention that it is great to have people love you and care for you, but it is even greater to love others and care for them. Talk with your child about ways she or he will care for someone this week. Emphasize our special Christian responsibility to care for the poor.

Conclude by having your child pray this prayer of the Church after you:

† Glory to the Father, and to the Son, and to the Holy Spirit. As it was in the beginning, is now, and will be for ever. Amen.

Learn by heart **Faith Summary**

- God knows and loves us.
- God made us to love one another.

Pray the Sign of the Cross with your family.

† In the name of the Father

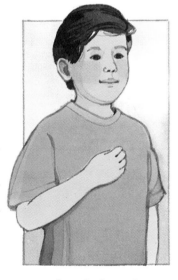

and of the Son

and of the Holy

Spirit.

Amen.

sticker

Circle the correct answer.

1. We are God's children.   Yes   No

2. There is only one God.   Yes   No

3. God does not know me.   Yes   No

4. There are three Persons in one God.   Yes   No

5. Tell how you will care for our world.

_____

_____

FAMILY SCRIPTURE MOMENT

As a family **Gather** and **Listen** to Luke's account of Jesus' baptism.

After all the people had been baptized, Jesus also was baptized. While He was praying, heaven was opened, and the Holy Spirit came down upon Him in bodily form like a dove. And a voice came from heaven, "You are my own dear Son. I am well pleased with You."
From Luke 3:21–22

Share Invite all to close their eyes and imagine that you are present at the baptism of Jesus. What will you say to Jesus? How will we follow Jesus' example of obedience?

Consider for family enrichment:

■ Jesus was baptized in the Jordan River by John the Baptist. John's baptism was not the sacrament of Baptism as we know it today. But it was a great event that marked the beginning of Jesus' public ministry, when He was affirmed by God and anointed by the Holy Spirit.

■ Soon after His baptism Jesus, the Son of God, began His work of proclaiming the kingdom, or reign of God.

Reflect and **Decide** Recall an experience of Baptism. Ask: What are our hopes for the one being baptized? What are our hopes for ourselves?

36

5 | God's Promise

Dear God, we know that You will love us always.

OUR LIFE

Read to me
A promise is a special thing
I say that I will do.
The reason that it's special is
I give my word to you.

A promise can be broken, but
I hope that mine won't be.
I want to be the kind of friend
Who keeps my word, you see.

Who are your friends?
Do you make promises to them?
Do you ever break your promises to them?

What does it mean to keep a promise?

SHARING LIFE

Choose a friendship partner.
Tell each other how it feels
to have a friend
who keeps promises.

Why should we
keep our promises?

OUR CATHOLIC FAITH

God's Promise

God promises to be with us
and to love us always.
Here is a Bible story that
helps us remember God's
promise of love.

Read to me from the Bible

The first man and woman lived in
a beautiful garden called Eden.
Their names were Adam and Eve.
God promised they would be happy
always if they did what He asked.
They had everything they needed.
But they still wanted more.

Adam and Eve turned away from
God. They did not do what God
asked them to do. This hurt Adam and Eve
and all their children. Then they felt
ashamed. So they hid from Him.
But God looked for them and found
them. He never stopped loving
them. God promised to send Someone to
help them.

From Genesis 2:8–3:15

God Keeps the Promise

God kept this promise by
sending us Jesus, God's own Son.
Jesus shows us how to love God
and one another.
If we live as Jesus shows us, we
can be happy with God forever.

We are the children of Adam
and Eve, too.
God wants us to choose
what is right.
Sometimes we do what
we should not do.
But God never stops loving us,
no matter what we do.
He promises to love us always.

COMING TO FAITH

What does God promise us?

Sit quietly and pray in your heart.
Think about God's promise.
Hold your right hand over your heart.
Tell God how you feel.
† Then say, "God, thank You
for loving me so much.
I will always love You."

PRACTICING FAITH

A rainbow is a sign to us
of God's promise of love.
Make a group "rainbow promise
banner." Put on your banner,
"God always loves us."

Hang your banner in the church
or parish center.
Invite the people at your church to
sign their names on your banner.
† Together pray, "Thank You, God,
for promising to love us always."

God Always loves us

Invite the children to share their faith
at home this week. Encourage them to
tell their families about the "rainbow
banner" and to invite their families to
come and sign it.

This week your child learned the biblical story of the creation of the first human beings. This story is not intended as a literal account of a historical event; it tells us, however, that God is our creator and that human beings lost the original gift of His friendship because of sin. As a result all human beings suffer the effects of this original sin.

God did not abandon the human race. He promised to send a Savior: "The Lord will give you a sign: a young woman is with child and will have a son whom she will call 'Immanuel'" (from Isaiah 7:14). Immanuel means "God is with us."

You might ask yourself:

■ *How has my faith enabled me to be a promise-keeping person, especially to my family?*

■ *This week how will our family show that we are grateful for God's faithful love?*

Use the activity below to talk with your child about the meaning of God's promise.

Keeping Promises

Spend some time talking together about times when your child finds it hard to keep a promise.

Learn by heart
Faith Summary

- People turned away from God.
- God promised to save us and gave us Jesus, His own Son.

Spread your arms wide like the rainbow. Say thank you for God's promise.

I will love you always.

From Jeremiah 31:3

41

First go over the *Faith Summary* with your child. Then have him or her complete the *Review*. The answers for questions 1–3 appear on page 200. The response to number 4 will help you find out the hurts in your child's life over promises she or he or others have broken. When the *Review* is completed, invite your child to put a sticker on this page.

Circle Yes or No.

1. Adam and Eve turned away from God.   Yes   No

2. God promises to be with us always.   Yes   No

3. God keeps His promises.   Yes   No

4. How do you feel when someone breaks a promise?

_____

_____

FAMILY SCRIPTURE MOMENT

Gather and **Listen** as a family.

One day when Jesus was praying alone, the disciples came to Him. "Who do the crowds say I am?" He asked them. "Some say that You are John the Baptist," they answered. "Others say that You are Elijah, while others say that one of the prophets of long ago has come back to life." "What about you?" He asked them. "Who do you say I am?" Peter answered, "You are God's Messiah."
From Luke 9:18–20

Share If you were present in this gospel scene, how would you respond to Jesus' question "Who do you say I am?"

Consider for family enrichment:
■ Luke depicts Jesus at prayer before He asks His disciples to express their faith in His true identity. Peter recognized Jesus as the Messiah, the Christ or Anointed One, sent by God to save God's people.
■ All of us must know and be able to answer who Jesus is for us and to proclaim Him as our Lord and Savior.

Reflect and **Decide** Imagine that Jesus is seated with your family right now. Tell Him how you will share your faith in Him with others. What will you say? What will you do? Ask Jesus to help you.

6 The Bible

God, open our
ears and hearts
to listen
to Your word.

OUR LIFE

Leader: Let us gather and quietly listen to very important words from the Bible, the book that is God's gift to us.

Reader: God says, "Be very quiet and listen to Me! Do not be afraid— I am with you!"

From Isaiah 41:1,10

All: God, listening to Your word makes us happy!

Reader: Jesus says, "Happy are those who do what God wants. He will bless them fully."

From Matthew 5:6

SHARING LIFE

How do you feel when you hear God say, "Do not be afraid—I am with you."? Tell about it.

OUR CATHOLIC FAITH

A long time ago some people wanted to tell God's story. They began by thinking about who made the world. They thought about who made them.

God helped the people to find answers to their questions. They wrote the story of all that God had done for them. We call God's story the Bible.

The stories in the Bible tell us about God and His love for us. We listen to God's story often, and we learn about His gifts to us.

The Bible tells us about God's best gift. God's best gift is Jesus Christ, His own Son.

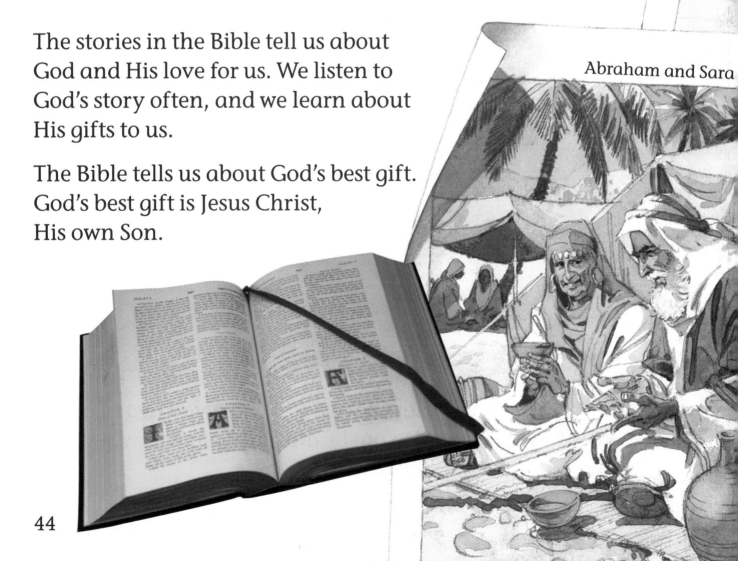

Abraham and Sara

Ruth

Palm Sunday

COMING TO FAITH

Let us share this song to tell God that we want to be good listeners to His word.
(To the tune of "If You're Happy")

♫ Oh, God, we're happy listening to Your word.
Oh, God, we're happy listening to Your word.
Oh, God, we give You glory
As we listen to Your story.
Oh, God, we're happy listening
to Your word. ♫

PRACTICING FAITH

Make a "Happy Listener" badge. Wear this badge when you listen to God's story in the Bible.

Wear your badge now as we carry the Bible to a special place.

Leader: Let us sing "Oh, God, We're Happy Listening to Your Word."

Leader: Let us pray with actions. Follow the pictures.

† **All:** God, listening to Your word makes us happy.

God, keeping Your word makes us happy.

God, sharing Your word makes us happy.

Talk with the children about ways they and their families might use the "Faith Alive" pages. Encourage them to share the prayer on their badges with their families.

46

FAITH ALIVE

AT HOME AND IN THE PARISH

In this lesson your child was introduced to a fuller understanding of the word of God in the Bible. The Bible is the word of God to us written in human language. The Second Vatican Council envisions a day when every Catholic will read, know, understand, and love the Bible. The Council urges us to pray over and meditate on the Bible as a primary source of spiritual growth and wisdom for daily life. If you do not already own a family Bible, you might want to get one now, read it often, and keep it in a place of honor in your home.

You might ask yourself:

■ *What will I do to develop and nourish a love for the Bible in my own life?*

■ *How might I help my child begin to develop a love for God's word in the Bible?*

God's Word at Mass

Remind your child of the responses we give to God's word at Mass. At the end of the first reading the reader says, "The word of the Lord." We answer, "Thanks be to God." After the gospel is read, we hear, "The gospel of the Lord." We answer, "Praise to You, Lord Jesus Christ." Help your child make these responses at Mass.

Learn by heart **Faith Summary**

- The Bible tells about God and His love for us.
- We listen carefully to God's message.

Here is the most important thing the Bible tells us.
Connect the hearts.

GOD loves us always.

47

sticker

Write the missing word on each line.

Jesus Christ   listen   love

1. God wants us to _____ to God's word.

2. The Bible tells us about God's _____ for us.

3. The Bible tells us that God's best gift to us is _____

_____ .

4. Tell a favorite story from the Bible.

FAMILY SCRIPTURE MOMENT

As a family **Gather** and **Listen** to God's word.

On the Sabbath Jesus went as usual to the synagogue. He stood up to read the Scriptures and was handed the book of the prophet Isaiah. He unrolled the scroll and found the place where it was written,

"The Spirit of the Lord is upon me,
because he has chosen me to bring good news to the poor.
He has sent me to proclaim liberty to the captives
and recovery of sight to the blind,
to set free the oppressed."

From Luke 4:16–18

Share What is Jesus saying to us in this passage? How do I respond?

Consider for family enrichment:

■ Note that Jesus looked for this text from Isaiah. It was the promise of the great jubilee year to benefit the poor and oppressed, to bring peace and justice for all.

■ This work of justice and peace is at the center of Jesus' ministry. As disciples, we must follow Jesus' example.

Reflect and **Decide** How will we as a family hear the word of God and reach out to those most in need?

7 All Saints

O God, we honor
all Your saints
today.

OUR LIFE

Read to me

All the children in the
neighborhood like Mr. Gorski. He
tells them stories and fixes their
broken toys. He lets them play in
his yard. He always talks with them
when they come to visit.

The children and their families
want to honor Mr. Gorski in a
special way. They are planning a
neighborhood party for him. The
day will be known as "Mr. Gorski's
Special Day."

Imagine you live in Mr. Gorski's
neighborhood. What would you
do for the party?

SHARING LIFE

Who is a special person you
would like to honor? Why?

How would you show that you
honor this person?

49

OUR CATHOLIC FAITH

In our Church we honor some special people each year on November 1. These special people are called saints.

Saints are people who love God and others very much. They did what God wanted them to do during their life on earth. Now they are happy with Him forever in heaven.

When they were alive, the saints tried to do the things Jesus told us to do,
• feed the hungry,
• help poor people,
• pray to God each day,
• share their things with others,
• be kind and fair to everyone,
• be peacemakers.

We do not know the names of all the saints who are with God in heaven. We celebrate the feast of All Saints to remember and honor all these special people.

Coming To Faith

Form two lines and face each other.
(Sing to the tune of "Do You Know the Muffin Man?")

♫ **Group 1**
Do you know Saint Elizabeth,
Saint Elizabeth, Saint Elizabeth?
Do you know Saint Elizabeth?
She fed the poor and hungry.

Group 2
Yes, we know Saint Elizabeth,
Saint Elizabeth, Saint Elizabeth.
Yes, we know Saint Elizabeth.
Saint Elizabeth, pray for us. ♫

Add to your song. Use these words
to honor these saints.

Saint Joseph
He cared for Jesus and Mary.

Saint Thérèse
She did little things for Jesus.

Saint Martin
He helped the sick and homeless.

Saint Nicholas
He helped the needy children.

Practicing Faith

How will you be like the saints?
How will you honor the saints
on November 1, All Saints' Day?
The pictures can help you decide.

Cut out the saints' cards on page 195.
Pray the prayer printed on the back.
Draw one of your favorite
saints on the empty card.
Share your cards with your
family and friends.

Talk with the children
about ways they and
their families might use
the "Faith Alive" pages.
Encourage them to invite
their families to continue
adding to their saints'
cards collection.

In this lesson your child developed a deeper appreciation of what it means to be a saint. As Catholic Christians we use the word saint to refer to those whose lives have been recognized by the Church as "holy or blessed." Saint Paul also used the word to include all those who have done and are doing God's will in their lives. A saint, then, is someone who truly lives the gospel teachings of Jesus Christ. The Second Vatican Council reminds us that all Christians are called by Baptism to such holiness of life.

On November 1, the Church celebrates the feast of All Saints, rejoicing in the holy lives of the countless but unknown saints throughout history. You might ask yourself:

■ *How does the Church's teaching about saints encourage me to live a holy life?*

■ *How might our family celebrate All Saints this year?*

Some Saints I Know

Your child has made some "saints' cards." Let your child share them with you and talk about each one. If possible, find out what you can about the saint for whom you named your child and tell the story to your child.

Learn by heart
Faith Summary

- Saints are people who loved God and did God's will on earth.
- We celebrate the feast of All Saints on November 1.

Me—a Saint!

Tell God how you try to be like the saints. Draw a picture to show one way you will do this.

sticker

Circle the correct word.

1. On November 1 we celebrate the feast of

_____.

Thanksgiving   All Saints   Christmas

2. _____ are people who lived as Jesus taught.

Saints   Everyone

3. Saints are now happy with God in

_____.

the Bible   heaven   my parish

4. Tell one thing you can do to live as Jesus taught.

FAMILY SCRIPTURE MOMENT

Gather and **Listen** to Jesus' amazing words:

Do not be afraid, little flock, for your Father is pleased to give you the kingdom. Sell all your belongings and give the money to the poor. Provide for yourselves purses that don't wear out, and save your riches in heaven, where they will never decrease, because no thief can get to them, and no moth can destroy them. For your heart will always be where your riches are.
From Luke 12:32–34

Share How do we feel about this advice from Jesus? Why do we feel that way?

Consider for family enrichment:
■ Jesus insists that His disciples trust in God rather than in material possessions. We must share with others and have a special care for the poor.
■ When our hearts are truly set on doing God's will, we need never be afraid.

Reflect Reread the words of Jesus. Ask: Where are our hearts right now? Name someone you know who is taking these words of Jesus to heart.

Decide How will we as a family or with other parishioners sell something we have and give to the poor?

54

UNIT 1 ▪ REVIEW

Creation is everything made by God.
God made the world and all things in it.
Everything He made is good.
God made all people wonderful
and wants them to care for all
living things.

God gives you His own life.
Grace is God's own life and
love in you. You can say,
"God is my loving Father.
I am His own child."

God knows and loves us.
There is only one God.
There are three Persons in God:
God the Father, God the Son,
and God the Holy Spirit.
The three Persons in God know
and love us.

God loves and cares for us always.
Sometimes we do what is wrong.
Even then, God loves and cares
for us.
God's greatest gift is Jesus, the
Son of God, who shows us how to
love God and one another.

UNIT 1 · TEST

Read to me

Color the happy face to say "Yes."

Color the sad face to say "No."

1. Everything God made is good.

2. I am God's own child.

3. The three Persons in one God know and love us.

4. Grace is not a special gift from God.

5. Tell about something you love that God gave you.

Child's name _____

Your child has just completed Unit 1. Have your child bring this paper to the catechist. It will help you and the catechist know better how to help your child grow in the faith.

_____ My child needs help with the part of the Review/Summary I have underlined.
_____ My child understands what has been taught in this unit.
_____ I would like to speak with you. My phone number is _____ .

(Signature)_____

Jesus, thank You
for being born
like us.

Our Life

Everyone was so happy
the day you were born!
Everyone said, "What a beautiful baby!

Welcome, _____."
                           (your name)

What do you know about the day
you were born?
Tell your story.

Sharing Life

Why are people happy when
a new baby is born?

Pretend you are talking
to Jesus when He was born.
What would you say?

The Story of Jesus

God wanted to give us the gift of Jesus.
Jesus is His own Son.
God asked Mary to be the mother
of Jesus
Mary said yes to God

From Luke 1:26–38

Read to me from the Bible
Mary was married to Joseph. They
went to a town called Bethlehem.
There was no room for them at the
inn. They had to stay in a stable.
There Mary gave birth to Jesus,
God's own Son. Mary laid Jesus in a
manger.
From Luke 2:4–7

We celebrate Jesus' birth at Christmas.

At **Christmas** we celebrate the birth of Jesus.

Jesus is one of us. He laughed and
played with His friends.
He loved and shared with them.
Sometimes He felt afraid and
got tired.

Jesus learned how to read.
He studied the Bible.
Mary and Joseph taught Him
to love and pray and work.
We call Jesus, Mary, and Joseph
the Holy Family.

Today Jesus is still part
of our human family.
Jesus helps our families to love
and care for one another as He did.

59

COMING TO FAITH

Imagine you are going to visit
the Holy Family for the whole day.
What might you do together?
What might you say to one another?
How would you feel?

PRACTICING FAITH

Pray in your heart. Ask Jesus, Mary,
and Joseph to help your family be a
holy family.

Color the prayer banner. Share the prayer
with your family. Invite your family to
write their names on it. Put your banner
where your family will see it every day
this week.

Holy Family
be with our family. Amen.

Take a few minutes to go
over the "Faith Alive"
pages with your children.
Encourage them to tell
the Christmas story to
someone at home.

FAITH ALIVE AT HOME AND IN THE PARISH

Trying to cope with bills, sickness, or family difficulties, you might have thought: Jesus never had problems like these. If you have thought this, you were wrong. We know from the Scriptures and the teaching of the Church that Jesus Christ, the Son of God, was one of us and shared our human condition. He was like us in all things but sin. This affirmation of the full humanity as well as the full divinity of Jesus Christ is a central dogma of our faith.

Jesus was born into a human family. We call Jesus, Mary, and Joseph the "Holy Family." Being a holy family does not mean that they did not share experiences familiar to us. The gospel records that Jesus Himself had to grow in "wisdom, age, and grace."

You might ask yourself:

■ *How can reflecting on the Holy Family help our family to grow in "wisdom, age, and grace"?*

■ *What action can we take this week to begin to make this happen?*

Use the activity below to talk with your child about how we can live as Jesus wants.

A Family Prayer
Here is a prayer you can pray with your family.

✝ Dear Jesus,
Help us to be a loving family.
Help us to be patient and kind.
Help us to reach out to those in need.
Thank You for being with us always.

Happy Feet

Color the music notes that tell ways you can help your family. On the line, write what you will do this week.

 **Faith Summary**

- Jesus is the Son of God.
- Jesus is one of us.

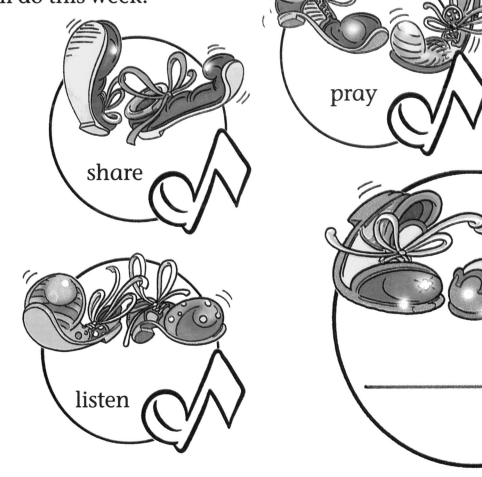

share

pray

listen

61

First go over the *Faith Summary* together. Then have your child complete the *Review*. The answers for questions 1–3 appear on page 200. The response to number 4 will help you see how close to Jesus your child feels. When the Review is completed, have your child choose a sticker to place on this page.

Write the missing word on each line.

Christmas   Jesus   Mary

1. **J**_____ is the Son of God.

2. We celebrate Jesus' birth at **C**_____.

3. God chose **M**_____ to be Jesus' Mother.

4. Tell how Jesus is your friend.

_____

_____

FAMILY SCRIPTURE MOMENT

Gather and **Listen** to the angel Gabriel's message to Mary as told by Luke: "Don't be afraid, Mary; God has been gracious to you. You will become pregnant and give birth to a son, and you will name Him Jesus. He will be great and will be called the Son of the Most High God. The Lord God will make Him a king, as His ancestor David was, and He will be the king of the descendants of Jacob forever; His kingdom will never end!"
From Luke 1:30–33

Share What do you hear the angel say to Mary?

How well do we respond to God in our lives?

Consider for family enrichment:
■ Jesus is a name that means "God saves us." Jesus is the Son of God and descendant of David, Israel's greatest king. Jesus is divine and human.
■ God chose Mary, a young woman without power, authority, or influence, to be the mother of Jesus. Her yes to God required great faith, trust, courage, and love.

Reflect and **Decide** What will we do this week to show that we are disciples of Jesus and give our yes to God, as Mary did? Seek Mary's help to follow Jesus by praying a Hail Mary together.

Jesus Is God's Own Son

OUR LIFE

Read to me

Yesterday was my dad's birthday. I wanted to show him how much I love him. But I had no money to buy him a gift.

Then I remembered a special rock I had in my treasure box. Dad and I found it on our walk one day. I rubbed the rock with oil to make it shine. I gave it to my dad at dinner.

After dinner Dad told me, "Your gift was my favorite. It really showed your love."

Name some things you treasure.

When would you ever give your treasure as a gift?

SHARING LIFE

Can love be a gift? Why?

Why is love the best gift of all?

What are some of the best gifts God gives us?

Jesus Is God's Own Son
God gives us many gifts.
His greatest gift to us is
Jesus Christ, the Son of God.

Jesus traveled from place to place
telling people about God's love.
He helped people in need.

Jesus showed people how much
God loved them.
He showed them how to love
and care for one another.
He taught them to care
for poor people in a special way.

What Jesus did and said showed
that He was the Son of God.

Read to me from the Bible
One day, Jesus and His friends were in a boat. Suddenly a strong wind began to blow. The waves began to fill the boat. Jesus' friends were afraid. Jesus stood up and told the wind and the sea, "Be quiet!" At once, the wind stopped blowing. The sea was quiet. The friends of Jesus said, "Who can this be that the wind and the sea obey him?"
From Mark 4:35–41

Jesus showed us in many ways what God is like.
He showed us by what He did and said.

Jesus said, "Anyone who has seen Me has seen the Father."

From John 14:9

COMING TO FAITH

Sometimes the captain of a boat has something important to tell. First the captain says on the loud speaker, "Now hear this!"

Take turns being the boat captain. Say, "Now hear this!" Then tell everyone something Jesus did or said to show us what God is like.

PRACTICING FAITH

Have a "Now hear this!" parade. Sing this song as you march. (To the tune of "Mary Had a Little Lamb")

♫ Jesus is God's gift to us,
Gift to us, gift to us!
Jesus is God's gift to us.
He is God's own Son.

Jesus shows God's love for us,
Love for us, love for us!
Jesus shows God's love for us,
He is God's own Son. ♫

Can you teach this song to someone at home?

"Now Hear This!"

For the children's participation in the "Faith Alive" activities, encourage them to teach their new song to someone at home.

10 Jesus Is Our Friend

Jesus, help us
to live as
Your friends.

Our Life

Read to me
I want to draw a picture of
The best friend there could be.
Here's what I'll put in the picture.
I hope you will agree.

A great big heart for loving,
And eyes to look and see;
I'll draw two ears for listening,
To be like you and me.

I'll add two hands for helping,
A mouth for smiling, too.
Now count the many special things
That your best friend can do!

Do you have a best friend?
What do you like to do together?

Sharing Life

Jesus wants to be your best friend.
How does that make you feel?

How can you be a good friend to Jesus?

Jesus Is Our Friend

Jesus loved and cared for everyone.
He hugged little children.
He healed people who were sick.
He helped people who were sad or afraid.
He cared especially for poor people.

Jesus cared for people who were
not easy to love.
He was fair to everyone.
He even loved those who hated Him.

Jesus said:
"Love your enemies.
Do good to those who hate you."

From Luke 6:27

Prayer is talking and listening to God.

Jesus is the best friend we can have.
Sometimes we feel alone or afraid.
But we are never really alone.
Jesus is always with us.

We can always talk or pray to Jesus.
We can tell Jesus we love Him.
We can thank Him for being
our best friend.

We can ask Jesus to help us and others.
If we do things that are wrong,
we can tell Jesus we are sorry.
Jesus always forgives us.

We can pray anywhere, anytime.
We can pray in the morning,
at night, or before we eat.

Jesus always hears our prayers.

COMING TO FAITH

Pray this new way.
Imagine that you are the child
on Jesus' lap.
Tell Jesus what you like best
about being His friend.

PRACTICING FAITH

Here is a prayer song to sing.
(To the tune of "Playmate")

♫ Jesus, my best friend,
Oh, You are always there.
You show me how to share,
You show me how to care.
Oh, You're my best friend,
I've learned what friends
   are for —
To love and share and care
Forever more! ♫

Now look at the pictures on
this page. Circle the ones
that show when you will pray
to Jesus.

Take time to go over the "Faith Alive"
activities with the children. Talk about
setting up a "prayer corner" at home.
Pray together the prayer on page 73.

In this lesson your child met Jesus as *healer*. Jesus befriended all kinds of people. They didn't have to be "religious" or "respectable." Jesus affirmed goodness in people from every walk of life. That is being a healer! One of the surest signs of Jesus' work of salvation was His healing touch. (Salvation comes from a word meaning "health.") He gave sight to the blind and hearing to the deaf, both in the literal and in the spiritual sense.

Most importantly, Jesus offered the healing touch of forgiveness of sins. Again and again He says, as He did to the paralyzed man, "Your sins are forgiven, my friend" (Luke 5:20). We experience the help and healing of Jesus today in the sacrament of Reconciliation, in the Eucharist, in the Christian community, in works of charity and justice, and in prayer.

You might ask yourself:
- *How do we reflect Jesus as healer in our family?*
- *How will we try to be more "healing" with one another?*

Prayer Corner

If possible, help your child to set up a prayer corner in his or her room. Place the Bible and pictures of Jesus and the Holy Family in the corner. Reserve a special time in the day when you and your child will go to this corner to pray.

Pray,

† Thank You, God, for giving us Jesus as our best friend. Amen.

Think of people who need Jesus' healing love.
Write each person's name on one of the sun's rays.
Ask Jesus to be with
him or her.

Learn by heart
Faith Summary
- Jesus cares for all people.
- We can pray to Jesus our friend.

Jesus, send your healing love.

First go over the *Faith Summary* together. Then have your child complete the *Review*. The answers for questions 1–3 appear on page 200. The response to number 4 will help you to find out whether your child needs more encouragement to talk to Jesus frequently. When the *Review* is completed, have your child choose a sticker for this page.

Write the missing word on each line.

healed   friend   pray

1. Jesus **h**_____ sick people.

2. We can always talk or **p**_____ to Jesus.

3. Jesus is my **f**_____ .

4. When do you like to pray?

_____

_____

FAMILY SCRIPTURE MOMENT

Gather and **Listen** to God's word.

Once Jesus was in a town where there was a man who was suffering from a dreaded skin disease. When he saw Jesus, he threw himself down and begged Him, "Sir, if You want to, You can make me clean!" Jesus reached out and touched him. "I do want to," He answered. "Be clean." At once the disease left the man.

From Luke 5:12–13

Share Do we turn to Jesus when we are sick and in pain? Why or why not? What do we expect of Him?

Consider for family enrichment:

■ Jesus healed many people as a way of drawing attention to the kingdom of God and as a sign that the Spirit of the Lord was upon Him.

■ One amazing feature of this story is that Jesus *touches* the leper, an act unheard of in Jesus' time.

Reflect Ask: Who are the "lepers" in our society? How are we to reach out to them?

Decide As a family, choose a sick person to whom you will show care this week.

11 Jesus Is Our Teacher

Jesus, teach
us to love.

Our Life

Read to me
In the school bus yesterday Lia taught me a hand game. Lia said, "Dad taught me last night. He said my grandmother taught it to him when he was our age."

Now I can't wait to show my cousin the next time I see him.

Talk about some good things your family has taught you.

What can you teach a friend?

Sharing Life

Do you like to learn new things from others? Why?

Do you like to share what you learn? Why?

Can you think of something Jesus has taught you?

75

Jesus taught people that God is
like a loving parent.
God loves us and cares for us,
no matter what we do.

One day Jesus' friends said,
"Teach us to pray."
Jesus said, "When you pray, call
God 'Father.' "
From Luke 11:1–2

Here is the prayer Jesus taught them.

✝ Our Father, who art in heaven,
hallowed be Thy name;
Thy kingdom come;
Thy will be done on earth
as it is in heaven.
Give us this day our daily bread;
and forgive us our trespasses
as we forgive those
who trespass against us;
and lead us not into temptation,
but deliver us from evil.
Amen.

The **Law of Love** teaches us to love God and others as we love ourselves.

The Law of Love

Jesus wants us to love God, and to love others as we love ourselves.

Read to me from the Bible

One day, a man came to Jesus.
He asked Jesus how God wants us to live.
Jesus said, "Love God above all things.
Love other people as you love yourself."
From Mark 12:29–31

This is how God wants us to live.
We call it the Law of Love.
We are to show our love for God
by loving others as we love ourselves.
What a happy world this would be
if we lived the great Law of Love!
Of all the good things that we can do,
Jesus said, love is the best thing of all.

Coming To Faith

Here are some ways Jesus taught us to love.

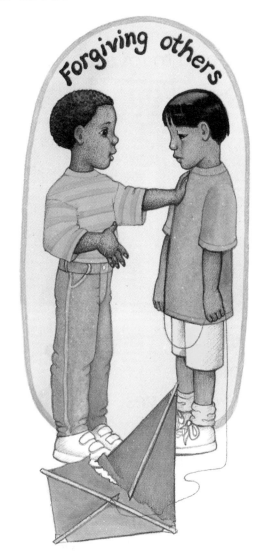

Join your hands in a circle.
Take turns going into the middle of the circle.
Act out how we can show love.
See if your friends can name each loving way.

Practicing Faith

Stay in your friendship circle.
Pray the Our Father together.

Pray this prayer at Mass with the people in your parish.
Practice saying the Our Father until you know it by heart.

78

Talk with the children about ways they might share the "Faith Alive" pages with their families. Pray the Our Father together as a closing faith response.

FAITH ALIVE AT HOME AND IN THE PARISH

In this lesson your child learned the great Law of Love. Jesus taught God's law that we must love God above all things and we must love others as we love ourselves.

Your child has also learned to pray the Our Father, the prayer that Jesus Himself taught. Help your child pray the Our Father often. It is a reminder of our need to love God above all and to love others as we love ourselves. The *Catechism of the Catholic Church* reminds us that the Lord's Prayer is a summary of the whole gospel.

You might ask yourself:

■ *When will we pray the Our Father together as a family?*

■ *How can our family show that we love others as we love ourselves?*

The Our Father

† Slowly pray the Our Father with your child. Then talk about each phrase to help your child to understand its meaning.

Learn by heart **Faith Summary**

- God is my loving Father.
- Jesus taught us the Law of Love.

Pray these words lovingly as you color the ribbon.

Our Father
who art in heaven
hallowed be Thy name.

Review
First go over the *Faith Summary* together. Then have your child complete the *Review*. The answers for questions 1–3 appear on page 200. Pay special attention to your child's response to number 4.

Talk about times when "friends" might encourage us not to be loving people as God wants. When the *Review* is completed, have your child choose a sticker for this page.

sticker

Write the missing word on each line.

Our Father   God   love

1. G_____is my loving Father.

2. Jesus taught us the O_____ F_____.

3. We must l_____ God, ourselves, and others.

4. Who teaches you to love God?

_____

_____

FAMILY SCRIPTURE MOMENT

Gather and **Listen** as Jesus speaks to us:

Ask, and you will receive; seek, and you will find; knock, and the door will be opened to you. For everyone who asks will receive, and the one who seeks will find, and the door will be opened to anyone who knocks.
From Luke 11:9–10

Share Invite family members to mime or act out what Jesus is advising us to do. Then ask: What is your understanding of His message for your life today?

Consider for family enrichment:

■ Luke's Gospel has many stories and sayings of Jesus teaching His disciples how to pray. Jesus encourages us to persevere in prayer, seeking God's blessing for ourselves and others.
■ God always responds to our prayers, although not always as we expect.

Reflect and **Decide** For what cause or person might we as a family ask, seek, and knock? What will be the special intention of our family prayer this week?

12 Jesus Gives Us Himself

Our Life

Some grandmas and grandpas
live far away.
Here are ways to tell them
we love them.

Phone a kiss.

Mail a hug.

Write a card.

Say a prayer.

Circle one you can do.
What else can you do?

Will it make your Grandma or
Grandpa happy?

Sharing Life

How do you remember
your friends when they
are away?

Does Jesus want you to
remember Him? Tell why.

Jesus Gives Us Himself

Jesus wanted us to remember Him.
Jesus wanted to be with us always.
This is what He did.

Read to me from the Bible

The night before Jesus died, He had
a special meal with His friends. We
call this meal the Last Supper.

During the meal, Jesus took bread.
He gave thanks to God. He broke
the bread. He gave it to His friends
and said, "This is My Body."

Jesus took a cup of wine. He gave
thanks again. He gave the cup to
His friends and said, "This is the
cup of My Blood."

The bread and wine became the
Body and Blood of Jesus.

Then Jesus said, "Do this in
memory of Me."

From Luke 22:14–20

We call this day
Holy Thursday.

Holy Communion is the Body and Blood of Christ.

The next day Jesus was nailed to a cross and died for us. We call this day Good Friday.

On Easter Sunday, God raised Jesus from the dead.

Jesus is with us today. Each time we go to Mass, He gives us the gift of Himself.

He gives us His Body and Blood. We call the Body and Blood of Jesus Holy Communion.

Coming To Faith

Imagine you and your friends are
at the Last Supper.
Tell what you hear Jesus say.

Then be very quiet.
Put your right hand over your heart.
Tell Jesus how you feel.

Practicing Faith

Listen at Mass for the story of
what Jesus did at the Last Supper.

Think of something to do this week
to thank Jesus for the gift of Himself.

Talk to the children about ways they
and their families might share the
"Faith Alive Pages." Then pray the
prayer in *Gifts for Mass* as a closing
faith response to this lesson.

FAITH ALIVE AT HOME AND IN THE PARISH

In this lesson your child learned about the Last Supper (Holy Thursday), the crucifixion and the burial of Jesus (Good Friday), and His resurrection (Easter Sunday).

This period from Holy Thursday evening to Easter Sunday evening is called the Easter Triduum. It is the high point of the Church's liturgical year. As you share the sacred events of the Triduum with your child, remember his or her age. As our children grow, they will share more deeply in the mystery of these days.

You might ask yourself:

■ *What will I do to become more aware of the presence of Jesus in my life? in my family's life?*

■ *How can I share my experience of Jesus in Holy Communion with my child?*

Gifts for Mass

Make a chart, like the one shown, for your kitchen. Ask each family member to draw a picture or a symbol for a gift of a good deed that each will give to Jesus at Mass next week. Some of the symbols shown below may be used.

Then talk with your child about the great love Jesus showed by giving His life for each of us. Say this prayer with your child:

† Thank You, Jesus, for giving us Yourself and for promising to help us always. Help us to give ourselves to others, especially to people in need.

Faith Summary
Learn by heart

- Jesus gives us the gift of Himself in Holy Communion.
- Jesus died and rose from the dead.

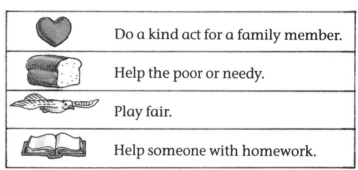

♥	Do a kind act for a family member.
🍞	Help the poor or needy.
🕊	Play fair.
📖	Help someone with homework.

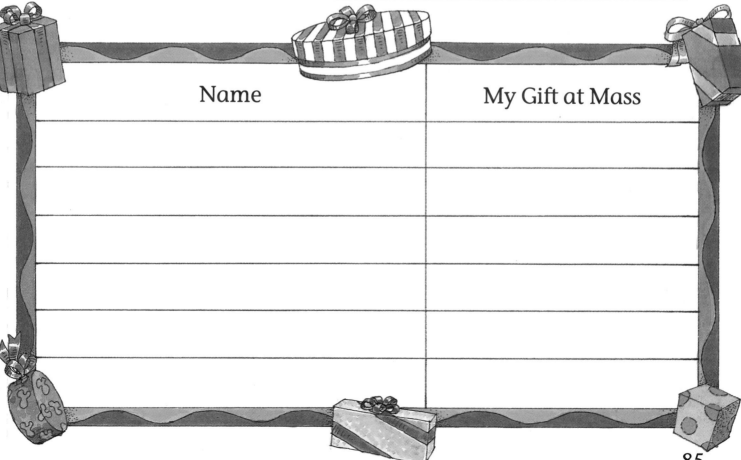

Name	My Gift at Mass

Review

First go over the *Faith Summary* with your child. Then have him or her complete the *Review*. The answers for questions 1–3 appear on page 200. Note the response to number 4 and help your child to follow through on his or her promise to

Jesus. When the *Review* is completed, have your child choose a sticker for this page.

sticker

Write the missing word on each line.

died   Jesus   Last Supper

1. Jesus gave us Himself at the L_____

S_____.

2. Holy Communion is the Body and Blood of

J_____.

3. Jesus d_____ for me.

4. What kind thing will I do to bring as a gift to Jesus?

FAMILY SCRIPTURE MOMENT

Gather and **Listen** to what happened when the risen Christ shared a meal with two disciples on the road to Emmaus.

Jesus sat down to eat with them, took the bread, and said the blessing; then He broke the bread and gave it to them. Then their eyes were opened and they recognized Him, but He disappeared from their sight. They said to each other, "Wasn't it like a fire burning in us when He talked to us on the road and explained the Scriptures to us?"
From Luke 24:30–32

Share How or when do we meet Jesus in our lives each day? Do we recognize Him? Why or why not?

Consider for family enrichment:
■ It was only in the breaking of the bread, the sign that Jesus had asked us to do in His memory, that these disciples recognized Him.
■ Do we recognize Jesus in each person we meet, as well as in the Eucharist?

Reflect and **Decide** If possible, read the entire story in Luke 24:13–35. Where will we look for the presence of Jesus this week? Is there someone for whom we will be a sign of the presence of the risen Christ?

13 Advent

Come,
Lord Jesus!

OUR LIFe

Read to me

Nana is coming
To visit tonight,
When the stars are out
And the moon is bright.

It's Nana's birthday
So we cleaned all day,
Getting ready for her
In a special way.

I'm so excited!
I can hardly wait!
When Nana's here,
We'll celebrate.

Do you ever help get ready
for a special celebration?
What do you do?

SHARING LIFe

What do you like best about celebrations?

How do you feel when you are waiting
to celebrate? Tell about it.

Do you remember the Bible story of the first man and woman? They turned away from God. But He did not stop loving them. God promised to send someone who would show people how to live as God's friends.

The people waited many, many years. God kept His promise by sending Jesus, the Son of God.

Each year we remember and celebrate Jesus' birth on Christmas. We continue to wait until Jesus will come again. Advent is the name we give to our waiting time before Christmas.

We do things to get ready for
the coming of Jesus. We pray to Jesus.
We light candles to remind us that
Jesus is our light. Jesus will come into our
hearts in a special way at Christmas.

Read the words of this Advent
message from the Bible.

Come, Jesus, come!
May the Lord Jesus
be with everyone.

Revelation 22:20–21

89

COMING TO FAITH

Sing this song during the four weeks of Advent. It will help you pray to Jesus as you get ready for Christmas.
(To the tune of "Twinkle, Twinkle")

♫ Jesus, Jesus, be our light.
Come to make the darkness bright.
Jesus, come and guide our way,
Help us care and share each day.
Jesus, Jesus, be our light.
Come to make the darkness bright. ♫

PRACTICING FAITH

How will you help and share in Advent? The pictures may help you decide.

Make an Advent calendar.
Color a star each day you do something to light the way for Jesus.

90

Talk to the children about ways they and their families might use the "Faith Alive" pages. Then sing the Advent song as a closing faith response.

In this lesson your child was introduced to the liturgical season of Advent as a time of waiting and preparing. For Catholic Christians, Advent has a dual purpose. It is a time to prepare for Christmas, when we recall and celebrate the first coming of God's Son. It is also a time to turn our minds to Christ's second coming, at the end of time. Advent, then, is a season of joyful and spiritual hope and of expectation for the "day of the Lord."

You might ask yourself:

■ *How does Advent challenge you to "prepare your heart"?*

■ *How can you help your family to prepare thoughtfully and prayerfully for Christmas?*

Learn by heart

Faith Summary

- Advent is a time of waiting to celebrate Jesus' birth at Christmas.
- We prepare for Christmas by praying and helping others.

Share the Advent song with your family and friends.

An Advent Song

(To the tune of "Twinkle, Twinkle Little Star")

Jesus, Jesus, be our light.
Come to make the darkness bright.
Jesus, come and guide our way,
Help us care and share each day.
Jesus, Jesus, be our light.
Come to make the darkness bright.

preparing for Christmas. When the *Review* is completed, have your child choose a sticker for this page.

Circle Yes or No.

1. God promised to send His Son to us.   Yes   No

2. We celebrate Jesus' birth at Easter.   Yes   No

3. During Advent we get ready for Jesus' birth at Christmas.   Yes   No

4. Tell something you will do to get ready to celebrate Jesus' birth.

_____

_____

_____

FAMILY SCRIPTURE MOMENT

Gather and **Listen** as a family.

Jesus said to the people, "When you see a cloud coming up in the west, at once you say that it is going to rain—and it does. And when you feel the south wind blowing, you say that it is going to get hot—and it does. Hypocrites! You can look at the earth and the sky and predict the weather; why, then, don't you know the meaning of this present time?"

From Luke 12:54–56

Share What signs can we detect that the season of Advent is here?

What is the meaning of this time for our family?

Consider for family enrichment:

■ Christians believe that Jesus will come again at the end of time to usher in the completion of the kingdom of God.

■ Jesus wants us to be alert for His final coming and ready for our own death.

Reflect What might Jesus be asking of our family through this reading from Luke?

Decide What special faith activity will we do as a family this Advent?

14 Christmas

Jesus,
we welcome You
into our hearts.

OUR LIFE

Sing "Silent Night" very softly.
We wish to welcome Jesus into our hearts.

♫ Silent night, holy night,
All is calm, all is bright;
Round yon Virgin Mother and Child!
Holy Infant so tender and mild,
Sleep in heavenly peace,
Sleep in heavenly peace. ♫

Tell about your feelings as you sing
this song.
What do the words of the song say
about the night Jesus was born?

SHARING LIFE

Imagine you are there in Bethlehem
on the first Christmas.
Tell what you see and hear.

93

A Christmas Play

Narrator: In those days, a letter went out from the king that all the people should be counted. Mary and Joseph went to Bethlehem to do this. Mary was expecting a baby.

Joseph: Mary, we are almost there. You must be tired. Let's stop at the inn. (knocks at the door)

Innkeeper: What do you want?

Joseph: We need a place to rest.

Innkeeper: There is no room for you here. You can stay in the stable in the back.

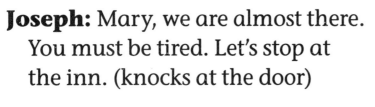

94

Narrator: So Joseph and Mary went to the stable. During the night, Jesus was born. Nearby shepherds were caring for their sheep. Suddenly a bright light filled the sky. Angels appeared to them.

Angels: Do not be afraid. We have good news. The Savior is born. You will find a baby in a stable in Bethlehem.

Narrator: The shepherds went to Bethlehem. They found Mary, Joseph, and the baby Jesus in the stable.

From Luke 2:1–16

Coming To Faith

Jesus came to bring us light and love. We want to share His light and love with others. Let us make a Christmas candle.

Gather around the Christmas crib, with your candle, as we pray.

✝ **Leader:** Welcome, Jesus, into our hearts today and always.
All: Welcome, Jesus, into our hearts.

Leader: Help us share the light of Your love with others.
All: Welcome, Jesus, into our world.

All: Sing "Silent Night" prayerfully.

PRACTICING FAITH

Jesus is with us today. How will you share
Jesus' light and love with others on
Christmas and every day?
Draw one of
the ways here.

Take a few minutes to
talk with the children
about ways they and
their families might use
the "Faith Alive" pages.
Encourage them to say
their Christmas promise
as a prayer during the
Christmas season.

FAITH ALIVE AT HOME AND IN THE PARISH

In this lesson your child was drawn into the Christmas story through music, prayer, and drama.

The birth of Jesus is not simply a historical event. It is a spiritual reality. Saint Francis of Assisi tells us that Jesus is, in a spiritual way, "born in each of us." Jesus lives in us through the good works we do and the Christian life we live. We are to make God present in our lives every day. In this sense the incarnation continues throughout history.

During the Christmas season, the Church celebrates the incarnation of the Son of God. The Church also celebrates the "epiphanies," or manifestations, of Christ to the magi and again at His baptism by John the Baptist.

You might ask yourself:

■ *How have our family celebrations of Christmas helped us remember that Christ is "born in each of us"?*

■ *How can you help your child to grow in this deeper meaning of Christmas?*

Learn by heart

Faith Summary

- Jesus was born in Bethlehem.
- Jesus wants us to share His love with others.

My Christmas Promise

Sign your name to show Jesus you want to remember this Christmas promise.

Jesus,
I will share Your light and love.

_____

Review

Go over the *Faith Summary* together before having your child complete the *Review.* The answers for questions 1–3 appear on page 200. The response to number 4 will help you see whether your child is growing in the understanding of Christmas. When the *Review* is completed, have your child put a sticker on this page.

Circle Yes or No.

1. There was room for Mary and Joseph at the inn.   Yes   No

2. Angels told shepherds about Jesus' birth.   Yes   No

3. Jesus was born in a stable.   Yes   No

4. Tell how you can share Jesus' love with a friend.

_____

_____

FAMILY SCRIPTURE MOMENT

Gather and share what each one likes about Christmas. Then **Listen** to the Christmas story.

Joseph went from the town of Nazareth in Galilee to the town of Bethlehem in Judea, the birthplace of King David. Joseph went there because he was a descendant of David. He went to register with Mary, who was promised in marriage to him. She was pregnant, and while they were in Bethlehem, the time came for her to have her baby. She gave birth to her first son, wrapped him in cloths and laid him in a manger—there was no room for them to stay in the inn.

Luke 2:4–7

Share What memories does the Christmas story stir up in us? How do we enter into the spirit of Christmas?

Consider for family enrichment:

■ Luke emphasizes that although Jesus was the Son of God, He was born in lowly surroundings.

■ So often Jesus can be "shut out" when the poor and homeless are neglected. To make room for Jesus now means to reach out to people most in need.

Reflect and **Decide** Sing a carol that communicates the Christmas message. Choose one way to serve the poor this Christmas.

SUMMARY 1 • REVIEW

God made all things.
God made the world wonderful.
He created plants, animals,
and people. People are special
in God's world. They can know
and love and make things.

God gave people a share in
His own life. This share in
God's life is called grace.

God always loves and cares for us
and wants us to love and care
for others.

Jesus is God's greatest gift to us.
Jesus is God's own Son.
He shows us how much
God loves us.
Jesus gave us the Law of Love.
He told us to love God, others,
and ourselves. Jesus is our
best friend.

Jesus died on Good Friday and
rose from the dead on Easter
Sunday. He is alive and with
us today.

SUMMARY 1 · TEST

Read to me

Circle the correct answer.

1. God _____ to be with us always.
   promises   hopes

2. _____ is God's own Son.
   Jesus   Joseph

3. The _____ tells God's story.
   Bible   Reader

4. God gives people _____ life.
   human   animal

5. There are _____ Persons in one God.
   four   three

6. We call God's own life in us _____.
   grace   life

7. Tell about one thing you will
   do to live the Law of Love.

Child's name _____

Your child has just completed Unit 2. Have
your child bring this paper to the catechist.
It will help you and the catechist know better
how to help your child grow in the faith.

_____ My child needs help with the part of the
        Review/Summary I have underlined.
_____ My child understands what has been
        taught in this unit.
_____ I would like to speak with you. My
        phone number is _____ .

(Signature)_____

15 The Holy Spirit

Our Life

The milk spilled.
The phone rang.
The baby cried.
The dog barked.

Everything happened
at the same time!
José's mother didn't know
what to do first.

"Don't worry, Mom," said José.
"I'll help you!"

Finish the story. Name some things that
José could do to help.

Tell about times when you help someone.

Sharing Life

Tell about a time when you needed
someone to help you.
Do you ever ask God for help?

101

The Holy Spirit Comes

Jesus knew that His friends
would need a Helper.
Jesus promised them,
"I will send you a Helper.
The Holy Spirit will help
you remember all that I have said."

From John 14:26

Here is the Bible story of how Jesus
kept His promise.

Read to me from the Bible

The friends of Jesus were waiting for the
Helper Jesus had promised. Mary, the
mother of Jesus, was with them.

Suddenly they heard a loud noise like
a wind blowing. They saw what looked
like flames of fire touching each one.

The Helper, the Holy Spirit, had come!
The friends of Jesus were filled with
God the Holy Spirit.

Then the friends of Jesus ran outside into
the street. They told all the people the
good news of Jesus.

From Acts 2:2–6

The **Holy Spirit** is God, the third Person of the Blessed Trinity.

God the Holy Spirit helped the friends of Jesus to remember everything Jesus had said and done.

The Holy Spirit helped the first Christians to tell everyone the good news of Jesus.

More and more people believed in Jesus Christ. They came together as Jesus' Church.

The Church is Jesus and His baptized friends joined together by the Holy Spirit.

The Holy Spirit helped the Church to begin. The Holy Spirit still helps the Church today to do the work of Jesus.

You are a follower of Jesus Christ. You are a member of His Church. The Holy Spirit helps you to live as a Christian, too.

103

Coming To Faith

Act out the story about how Jesus kept
His promise to send the Holy Spirit.

What help did the Holy Spirit
give the first Christians?

How can the Holy Spirit help you today?

Practicing Faith

Close your eyes. Imagine you are the
streamers in the picture. Stand still
waiting for the wind. Then flutter and fly
gently in the wind.

Sway back and forth or twirl around.
Pray to the Holy Spirit as you move.

† Holy Spirit, help me today
in all I think and do and say!

Will you say this prayer each day
this week?

Talk with the children
about ways they and
their families might use
the "Faith Alive" pages.
Encourage them to share
their Holy Spirit prayer
with someone at home.

FAITH ALIVE AT HOME AND IN THE PARISH

Of the three Persons of the Blessed Trinity, perhaps the third Person is the least understood and the most neglected in the practice of our faith.

The difference that the Spirit can make in our lives becomes abundantly clear when we consider how Pentecost transformed the apostles. After the death of Jesus, the disciples were filled with doubt, fear, and self-recrimination. But when the Holy Spirit came upon them, they were filled with confidence and courage. They proclaimed openly and fearlessly their faith in Jesus.

You might ask yourself:

■ *How often do I speak with my family about ways the Holy Spirit can bring comfort, peace, and happiness?*

■ *How will my family and I turn to the Holy Spirit as our Helper this week?*

Use this activity to talk with your child about ways the friends of Jesus showed their love for one another after they were filled with the Holy Spirit.

Invite your child to talk about times when he or she might need the help of the Holy Spirit. Then say this prayer together:

† Come, Holy Spirit, help us to remember what Jesus said and did. Help us to live as Christians. Help us to tell the good news of Jesus by what we say and by the way we live. Amen.

Learn by heart

Faith Summary

- The Holy Spirit came to the friends of Jesus.
- The Holy Spirit helped the Church to begin and helps us today.

Pray to the Holy Spirit.

HOLY SPIRIT

Help me today in all I think and do and say!

Color the circle next to the best answer.

1. The Holy Spirit helps all _____.

○ Christians   ○ animals   ○ plants

2. The Holy Spirit helps Jesus' friends to _____.

○ fight   ○ eat   ○ be peacemakers

3. A _____ is a follower of Jesus Christ.

○ Holy Spirit   ○ Christian   ○ friend

4. Tell how you will help someone today.

FAMILY SCRIPTURE MOMENT

Gather and **Listen** as a family.

At that time Jesus was filled with joy by the Holy Spirit and said, "Father, Lord of heaven and earth! I thank You because You have shown to the unlearned what You have hidden from the wise and learned. Yes, Father, this was how You were pleased to have it happen."
From Luke 10:21

Share Recall times when family members have been filled with joy and enthusiasm by the Holy Spirit. Ask: Why were we joyful? Why do you think Jesus is joyful in this reading?

Consider for family enrichment:

■ This reading follows the return of seventy-two disciples who had been sent on missionary journeys. Jesus rejoices that God's kingdom has been made known through these "everyday people."

■ We do not need special credentials to live the Christian life. But we do need to be open to the guidance and help of the Holy Spirit.

Reflect and **Decide** To what ministries might the Spirit be calling us in our parish? In our family?

16   The Church Is for Everyone

Jesus, how good it
is to belong
to Your Church!

Our Life

Look at the picture of all the animals working together.

What do you think they are trying to do?

How is each animal helping?

Do you like to work with others?

What team or group do you belong to?

What do you do?

Sharing Life

Why do people sometimes need to work together?

Why should friends of Jesus work together?

OUR CATHOLIC FAITH

We Belong to Jesus' Church

Jesus wants us to love God and to live as His followers. Jesus said, "Love one another just as I have loved you."
John 15:12

When Jesus saw that people were hungry, He fed them. If people were sad, He became their friend.

When Jesus saw sick people, He helped them. He cared about poor people. Jesus was fair to everyone. He helped people to live in peace.

We are followers of Jesus Christ. We are Christians. We belong to the Church.

We try to live as Jesus did. We try to show our love for one another. This is what it means to be followers of Jesus.

Jesus invites everyone to belong to His Church. Everyone in the Church is important.

People serve the Church in different ways. The first leaders of the Church were the apostles. Our Holy Father, the pope, is the leader of the whole Catholic Church. The pope and the bishops lead us in the same way as the apostles did. Priests and deacons serve the Church with them.

Many other people serve the Church, too. Think of all the people who help in your parish.

All of us together help care for the Church. We help one another live as followers of Jesus Christ.

COMING TO FAITH

Who is the leader
of the whole Church?

Can you name someone
else who helps the Church?
What does this person do?

Tell how you feel about
belonging to the Church.

PRACTICING FAITH

Tell what you will do
if each of these happens:

A classmate forgets lunch.

A new classmate
is lonely and afraid.

Someone is calling
someone else bad names.

Your younger brother
or sister wants you to play.

Tell what you will do today
to show that you follow Jesus.

Talk to the children about ways they
and their families might use the "Faith
Alive" pages. Encourage them
especially to do the *Praying Together*
Activity.

110

FAITH ALIVE AT HOME AND IN THE PARISH

This week your child learned how we are to live as Jesus' followers in God's special family, the Church, and how we are to follow the Law of Love. One way to help young children grow as committed members of the Church is to try to provide them with a family life balanced in work, prayer, and play.

Such balance is especially challenging in our culture today. Sometimes families are unhappy because they do not always keep a regular schedule. Children can become confused and upset when they do not eat, sleep, study, and play at the same times each day. Moreover they may become selfish if family members do not model care for one another with definite jobs and responsibilities. Children must be taught the value of working together. This is essential formation for living the Christian life.

You might ask yourself:

■ *How does my family try to live the Law of Love that my child learned about this week?*

It might be fun to create a weekly chart that shows the times for bed, meals, and so on. The chart could also list each person's weekly tasks with room for each one to check when it has been done satisfactorily. Plan a family treat for the weekend after each one has done the weekly tasks well.

Use the activity below to talk with your child about ways Jesus' friends help one another.

Praying Together

Share with your child a prayer of thanks for belonging to the Church. You may wish to use the following prayer:

† Jesus, thank You for inviting me to belong to Your Church. Help me and my family to do our part by following Your way.

Learn by heart **Faith Summary**

- Jesus invites everyone to belong to His Church.
- We are part of the Church and try to treat others as Jesus did.

As you color each bead, say the prayer to Jesus on the clasp.

Jesus, I am your friend.

111

sticker

Color the circle next to each correct answer.

1. The leader of the whole Church is the _____.

◯ bishop   ◯ pope   ◯ priest

2. We belong to the _____.

◯ circus   ◯ sea   ◯ Church

3. The Church of Jesus is for _____.

◯ Paul   ◯ everyone   ◯ no one

4. How will I be a follower of Jesus this week?

FAMILY SCRIPTURE MOMENT

Gather and **Listen** as Jesus tells us one of His parables about the kingdom of God.

Jesus asked, "What is the kingdom of God like? What shall I compare it with? It is like this. Someone takes a mustard seed and plants it in his field. The plant grows and becomes a tree, and the birds make their nests in its branches."
From Luke 13:18–19

Share what each one hears from this parable for his or her life.

Consider for family enrichment:

■ Jesus frequently told stories and parables about the kingdom of God. It was His central message. Like the mustard tree, the kingdom is to grow so that all people can make their home within its welcoming branches.

■ We help the kingdom grow when we "water" it with prayer, worship, and works of justice, peace, and mercy.

Reflect Reread the parable. Ask: What do we hear for our lives now?

Decide Choose something to do as a family this week to bring about the kingdom in our family and in our parish.

112

Our Life

Read to me

Janie watched the priest place Anthony
in the water. She listened to all the words.
When the Baptism was over, the priest
said, "Anthony is now a child of God.
Let us welcome him into the Church."
Everyone clapped. Janie's mother turned
to her and said, "Janie, you are
a child of God too."

Janie was excited.
"I'm a child of God, too!" she said.

Can you tell how you feel
about being a child of God?

Sharing Life

Tell why you think
your family wanted you to
become a child of God.

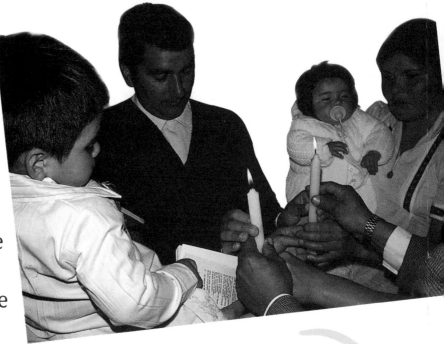

Baptism Makes Us God's Children

Jesus wants everyone to be a child of God.
He wants everyone to have God's own life and love.

When we are baptized, we become God's own children.
We receive God's own life and love. We call this grace.
We become part of the Church.

Catholic parents want their babies to become children of God through Baptism.
They bring their babies to their parish church.
The priest and the people welcome and pray for them.

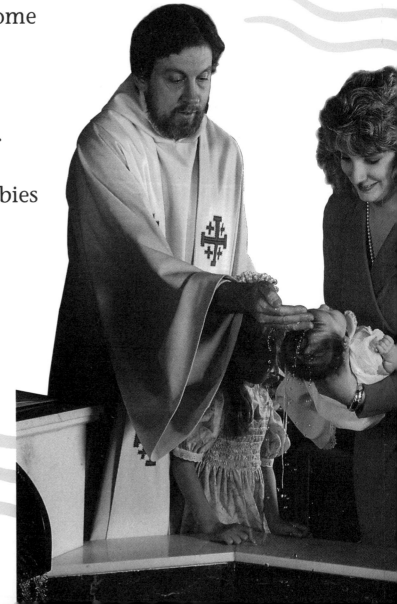

114

Baptism gives us grace, God's own life and love.

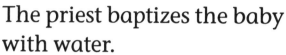

The priest baptizes the baby with water.
He says, "I baptize you in the name of the Father, and of the Son, and of the Holy Spirit."

The baby now has God's life of grace. The baby is a child of God and a member of Jesus' Church.

You are baptized.
You share in God's life and love.
You are God's child because you share in His grace.
You belong to the Church.

The Holy Spirit is with you.
The Holy Spirit helps you to live as Jesus taught us.

From John 14:16–17

WE ARE GOD'S CHILDREN

COMING TO FAITH

Imagine a friend asks you,
"What does it mean to be baptized?"
What would you say?

PRACTICING FAITH

We will celebrate being children of God.
Let us stand and clap for each other.
Bow to the person on each side of you.
Now make the sign of the cross
as you are sprinkled with holy water.
This will remind you of the day you
were baptized.

Pray together,
✝ Thank You, God, for making us Your
children in Baptism.

What can you do this week to show
you are a child of God?

116

Talk to the children about
ways they and their fami-
lies might use the "Faith
Alive" pages. Use the
suggested reflective
prayer on page 117 as a
closing faith response.

FAITH ALIVE AT HOME AND IN THE PARISH

Memories are very important to a child. Telling your child the story of her or his own Baptism, especially your family's joy on that day, will help your child feel happy about being a child of God.

The next time you take your child to church, point out the place of Baptism (immersion pool or font). Explain how each of us as baptized persons has the responsibility to live each day as a follower of Jesus and to carry on His work. This does not mean doing only extraordinary things, but rather the small, everyday things as best we can. It means caring especially for those in need and those who are treated unjustly. Your example in living out your own baptismal witness will help your child in living the Catholic Christian faith.

You might ask yourself:
■ *What does Baptism mean to me in my daily life?*

Act out with your child his or her Baptism. Then have your child do the activity below.

A Family Prayer

Talk with your child about God's life within us. Teach him or her to reflect quietly on this wonder of God's love. You might like to lead your child in the following reflective prayer.

Close Your Eyes

† Think quietly for a few minutes about God's life in you. Then give thanks in your own words for this wonderful gift. Then pray for help to share this gift with others.

Learn by heart
Faith Summary

- We share in God's own life when we are baptized.
- Baptism makes us children of God and members of Jesus' Church.

I Am God's Child

How do you grow as God's child?
Write your name or put yourself in the flower.
Think quietly about God's life in you.
Thank God for this wonderful gift.

Review

First go over the *Faith Summary* with your child. Then have him or her complete the *Review.* The answers for questions 1–4 appear on page 200. The response to number 5 will show you whether your child is beginning to understand what it means to live as a child of God. When the *Review* is completed, have your child choose a sticker to place on this page.

Color the circle next to each correct answer.

1. You became God's child at _____.

○ Baptism   ○ born   ○ singing

2. The Church uses _____ to baptize.

○ sand   ○ water   ○ sugar

3. Because we are baptized, we live like _____.

○ plants   ○ birds   ○ Jesus

4. In Baptism we receive God's own _____.

○ cross   ○ life   ○ body

5. What will you do this week to show you are God's child?

FAMILY SCRIPTURE MOMENT

Gather and discuss what you think Jesus' attitude was towards small children. Then **Listen** to this beautiful story about Jesus and the children.

Some people brought their children to Jesus for Him to place His hands on them. The disciples saw this and scolded them for doing so, but Jesus called the children to Him and said, "Let the children come to Me and do not stop them, because the kingdom of God belongs to such as these. Remember this! Whoever does not receive the kingdom of God like a child will never enter it."
From Luke 18:15–17

Share What did we hear in this reading for our lives?

Consider for family enrichment:

■ Belonging to the kingdom of God demands a childlike trust. Adults should not think that they can gain the kingdom simply by effort or brainpower!

■ Childlike does not mean "childish." We are to place our faith and trust in God as children would a loving parent.

Reflect Ask: What does it mean for me to accept the kingdom of God as a child would?

Decide on something to do to celebrate and cherish the child in each family member.

18 The Church Celebrates
(The Mass Begins)

OUR LIFE

The animals have finished helping
the beavers build a dam.
They have decided to celebrate.

Tell what you think each animal
did to get ready for the celebration.

What is your family's favorite
celebration? How do you help?

SHARING LIFE

Imagine the best celebration ever.

Who would be there?

What would there be to eat?

What would you wear?

What would you do?

We Gather to Celebrate

The Mass is the great celebration
that Jesus gave us.
Everything about it is special.

Jesus is with us each time
we celebrate the Mass.
We gather with our family
and friends. We come together
in our parish church
on Saturday evening
or on Sunday.

We celebrate Mass
together as Jesus' friends.
The priest leads our parish
community at Mass.

We gather around
a special holy table.
We call this table the altar.

A special plate and cup
are used for the bread and wine.
The plate is called the paten.
The cup is called the chalice.

The **Mass** is the special celebration in which we hear God's word, remember Jesus' dying and rising, and share the Body and Blood of Christ.

Everyone has something to do at Mass. This shows we are all God's people. To begin Mass we stand together and sing.

With the priest, we make the sign of the cross. We hear the priest say, "The Lord be with you." We answer, "And also with you."

We ask God and one another for forgiveness. Then we join with the priest to tell God how wonderful He is. We get ready to listen to God's word when it is read from the Bible.

121

COMING TO FAITH

Tell about each of these ways
we celebrate at Mass.

      sing   pray   listen

What can you do to join in the Mass?
Tell why you like doing this.

PRACTICING FAITH

Jesus invites you and your family to gather
at Mass with your parish family.
Answer Jesus' invitation by finishing this
letter to Jesus.

Dear Jesus,
   I will try to join with
my parish family at Mass
this weekend. I will thank
God for _____

_____

_____

_____

_____

Take a few minutes to
talk with the children
about ways they and
their families might use
the "Faith Alive" pages.
Encourage them to
make their *My Mass
Book* (pages 181–184)
and to share it with
their families.

FAITH ALIVE AT HOME AND IN THE PARISH

Some children and adults find Mass boring because they do not appreciate what the Eucharist celebration means. All that we are and do as Catholics should lead to and flow from the liturgy. Each of the other sacraments is connected to and directed toward the Eucharist. All Catholic Christians should be able to find in the weekly liturgy a source of nurture in Christian living.

We can strengthen our family's appreciation of the Mass by good preparation. For example:

■ explaining what will happen at Mass;

■ reading and reflecting on the readings for the liturgy;

■ asking each family member to do one good deed each day as a special gift to bring to Jesus at Mass.

Ask your child what good deed she or he would like to bring to Jesus at Mass this week. Talk about it together. Then have your child complete the activity below.

Mass Booklet

On pages 181–184 of your child's religion book, you will find *My Mass Book*. Help your child make this booklet and encourage him or her to use it at Mass.

Learn by heart Faith Summary

- Jesus is with us each time we celebrate the Mass.
- We all have a part to play in the Mass.

Draw the gift you will bring to Jesus.

Color the circle next to each correct answer.

1. Jesus is with us each time we celebrate _____.

◯ the Mass   ◯ breakfast   ◯ hockey

2. The special Mass table is the _____.

◯ altar   ◯ candle   ◯ cross

3. Our leader at Mass is the _____.

◯ teacher   ◯ priest   ◯ me

4. Tell about your favorite way of taking part in the Mass.

FAMILY SCRIPTURE MOMENT

Gather and **Listen** as Jesus speaks to us:

So watch what you do! If your brother sins, rebuke him, and if he repents, forgive him. If he sins against you seven times in one day, and each time he comes to you saying, "I repent," you must forgive him.
From Luke 17:3–4

Share How do you feel about this challenging teaching of Jesus to forgive always, no matter what?

Consider for family enrichment:

◼ In the Bible, the number seven means without limit. There should be no end to our forgiving others.

◼ We forgive others because we trust that God forgives us. We pray "forgive us our trespasses…."

Reflect Ask family members to recall in silence one thing for which they have not forgiven others fully, and to imagine what they will do about it.

Decide Pray together for Jesus' healing power of forgiveness. Pray the Lord's Prayer (or Our Father) together and share a sign of peace.

19 The Church Celebrates
(The Mass Continues)

OUR LIFE

Read to me

Megan called her aunt to tell her exciting news. "Aunt Sondra, guess what! Last Sunday at Mass Dad, Mom, Jessie, and I carried up the gifts of bread and wine to the altar."

Aunt Sondra answered, "Oh, what an honor! Megan, how did you feel?"

Megan told her aunt, "At first I was afraid because everybody would be watching us. But then Dad told me that we were bringing up the gifts for everybody there. I felt very special. I hope we get to do it again."

Would you like to bring up the gifts at Mass? Why or why not?

SHARING LIFE

What is your favorite way to take part in the Mass? Tell about it.

OUR CATHOLIC FAITH

We Listen to God's Word

At Mass we listen to God's word.
We try to be good listeners.

When the reader says,
"The word of the Lord,"
We answer,
"Thanks be to God."

Then we listen to the gospel.
The gospel is the good news,
or stories, of Jesus.

After the gospel, the deacon or priest
says, "The gospel of the Lord."
We answer,
"Praise to you, Lord Jesus Christ."

We sit and listen quietly. The priest
talks to us about the readings
from the Bible.

Then we pray a prayer that tells
what we believe.
We call this our Creed.

After this, we pray for all people.
After each prayer we answer,
"Lord, hear our prayer."

The **gospel** is the good news of Jesus.

Our Gifts to God Become Jesus

Some people bring our gifts of bread and wine to the altar.

The priest prepares our gifts to be offered to God. We pray, "Blessed be God forever."

During the Thanksgiving Prayer, the priest takes the bread in his hands. He prays in the name of Jesus, "This is my body which will be given up for you."

He takes the cup of wine and says, "This is the cup of my blood."

The bread and wine become Jesus Himself through the words and actions of the priest.

At the end of Mass the deacon or priest says,
"Go in peace to love and serve the Lord."

We answer,
"Thanks be to God."

We go in peace to love and serve God and one another.

127

COMING TO FAITH

What happens to our gifts of bread and wine at Mass?

Tell about your favorite part of the Mass.

Why is it your favorite?

PRACTICING FAITH

Look at the pictures of the Mass in this lesson. Tell what is happening in each picture.

Put yourself in one of the pictures. Tell what you will do to take part next time you go to Mass.

Talk to the children about ways they and their families might use the "Faith Alive" pages. Encourage the children to ask someone at home to go over the Mass responses with them so that they will be able to respond at Mass.

FAITH ALIVE AT HOME AND IN THE PARISH

In this lesson your child continues to learn what happens during Mass. The better we parents understand the Mass, the more we can help our children to appreciate it. It is important that we realize that Jesus is truly present to us in the Liturgy of the Word, preparing us for communion with Him in the Liturgy of the Eucharist. Having been reconciled and nourished by the word, we are called to the Lord's Supper in the Liturgy of the Eucharist. Along with the bread and wine, we offer ourselves to God as a living sacrifice of gratitude and praise.

During the Eucharistic Prayer, the bread and wine become the Body and Blood of Christ. This is done through the words and actions of the priest and the power of the Holy Spirit. In Holy Communion, we are united with Jesus Christ and with one another as members of Christ's Body in the world.

Renewed by the Eucharist, we are called to try to be "bread of life" for others—especially the poor, the suffering, and those who have been deprived of life and love.

Mass Booklet

Continue helping your child use the Mass booklet from text pages 181–184 during Mass.

Learn by heart **Faith Summary**

- We listen to God's word at Mass.
- Our gifts to God become Jesus, whom we receive in Holy Communion.

Lord, hear our prayer.

I Join in the Mass

Draw yourself with the people at Mass. Then say the response prayer.

sticker

Color the circle next to each correct answer.

1. The _____ is the good news of Jesus.

○ singing   ○ gospel   ○ loving

2. The prayer that tells what we believe is the

○ Our Father   ○ Creed   ○ Hail Mary

3. At Mass the bread and wine become ____.

○ Mary   ○ Jesus   ○ Paul

4. How will you try to be a peacemaker this week?

FAMILY SCRIPTURE MOMENT

Gather and **Listen** as Jesus tells us about a woman He admires.

Jesus looked around and saw rich men dropping their gifts in the Temple treasury, and He also saw a very poor widow dropping in two little copper coins. He said, "I tell you that this poor widow put in more than all the others. For the others offered their gifts from what they had to spare of their riches; but she, poor as she is, gave all she had to live on."

From Luke 21:1–4

Share Have family members imagine that they are the widow in the story. Ask: To whom would you be so generous? Why?

Consider for family enrichment:

■ Jesus loves the widow because she gives the little she has while trusting that God will provide for her.

■ The widow is a more faith-filled person than the rich people who give from their excess wealth and find their security in material possessions.

Reflect What might our family do this week to respond to Jesus' challenge in this story?

Decide Pray together: Loving God, give us a generous heart toward those most in need.

130

Jesus, help me
spend quiet
prayer time
with You.

Our Life

Read to me
Shelly Turtle had many friends in the bayou.
She loved to talk with them and help them.

One morning, she was sitting in the sun.
Her friends Gator and Froggie wanted
her to play. But Shelly said, "Not right now!
I need some quiet time. I'm just going
to go inside, relax, and think."

Gator asked, "How about this afternoon?"
Shelly answered, "That would be great!
See you later, Gator!"

Do you sometimes like to take
time out for quiet time alone?
When do you do this?

Sharing Life

Do you like to talk to God
during quiet time? Why?

How does it feel to talk to God?
Tell how this helps you.

Jesus teaches us that we need quiet time.
He spent quiet time praying to God.
He went to the desert and hills
to talk and listen to God.

Lent is a special time to pray and to grow
in love for Jesus. We talk and listen to
Jesus, our best friend, in quiet time.
We remember Jesus died for us.
We remember Jesus rose from the dead
to give us new life.
We thank Jesus for all He did for us.
We thank Jesus for His love.
We tell Jesus how much we want to
grow in love for Him.
We ask Jesus to help us share His love
with others, especially those in need.

We remember that Jesus said, "Love one
another, just as I love you."

From John 15:12

Coming To Faith

Think of ways you can take time to grow as a friend of Jesus. Here is one way to pray in your heart during Lent.

Be still like a turtle inside its shell. If you want to, close your eyes. Feel the love of Jesus all around you. Imagine you hear Jesus say, "You are My friend. Talk to Me."

✝ Jesus, I want to tell You …
Jesus, I want to thank You …
Jesus, I was wondering …
Jesus, help me to grow in …
Jesus, help me to share …

133

PRACTICING FAITH

Imagine you hear Jesus say, "Go, My friend. Help others to grow in their love for Me."

How will you do this during Lent? The pictures on this page may help.

Make signs for your door to help you tell others how you are spending time — alone or with others — in Lent.

Talk to the children about ways they and their families might use the "Faith Alive" pages. Encourage the children to share quiet prayer time with their families during Lent.

FAITH ALIVE AT HOME AND IN THE PARISH

In this lesson your child was introduced to the liturgical season of Lent as a special time for prayer and good works. It is a time of preparation for the most important moments of the Church year—the remembrance and celebration of the life, death, and resurrection of Christ. Lent should be a positive experience for your child, not a negative one. It is also a time when we are especially one with those preparing to be initiated into the Church during the Easter Vigil.

The Church encourages us to prepare in a spirit of loving self-sacrifice by praying and studying Scripture, by fasting, by giving alms to the poor, and by ministering to those in need.

You might ask yourself:

■ *What aspect of my life should I review during this Lenten season?*

■ *How can I help my child participate—at an appropriate level—in the family's Lenten observance?*

You can begin by doing this activity with your child.

Faith Summary

Learn by heart

- Lent is a special time to grow in love for Jesus.
- We remember that Jesus died for us and rose from the dead.

A Place to Pray

Finish the picture of a place where Jesus prayed.
Imagine you are with Jesus there.
When you pray during Lent, picture yourself in this place with Jesus.

135

Review

Go over the *Faith Summary* together. Then have your child complete the *Review.* The answers for questions 1–3 appear on page 200. The response to number 4 will help you find out whether your child has a growing understanding of Lent. When the *Review* is completed, have your child place a sticker on this page.

Write the correct answer.

Lent   love   pray

1. Jesus wants us to grow in His _____ .

2. _____ is a special time to do this.

3. We _____ to Jesus for help.

4. Tell one way you will try to grow in love.

_____

_____

FAMILY SCRIPTURE MOMENT

Gather and **Listen** as a family.

One of the criminals hanging there hurled insults at Jesus: "Aren't you the Messiah? Save yourself and us!" The other one, however, rebuked him, saying, "Don't you fear God? You received the same sentence He did. Ours, however, is only right, because we are getting what we deserve for what we did; but He has done no wrong." And he said to Jesus, "Remember me, Jesus, when you come as King!" Jesus said to him, "I promise you that today you will be in paradise with Me."
From Luke 23:39–43

Share What do we learn for our own lives from Jesus' forgiveness of the "good thief"?

Consider for family enrichment:

■ The "good thief" wins Jesus' admiration because he trusts totally in God. With faith, the thief recognizes Jesus as the Son of God who assures him of God's mercy.

■ Lent is a special time for offering and receiving forgiveness.

Reflect and **Decide** Have each person tell the personal lesson learned from this story. How will we renew our confidence in Jesus' forgiveness this week?

21 Easter

Alleluia, Jesus!
We have good
news to tell!

Our Life

What words do you say
when you are excited or very happy?

How do they help you tell
others how you feel?

Sharing Life

Celebrate and share Easter
good news.

Act out the prayer words.

† God, Your world says Alleluia!
Birds fly from tree to tree
and chirp in early morning.
Frogs hop near the pond
and croak. Butterflies quietly
flutter their wings.

Bees dance upon the flowers
opening in sunlight.
They buzz happily.

And I jump for joy and say,
"Alleluia! We celebrate Jesus'
new life."

An Easter Play

Narrator: Mary Magdalene was crying outside of Jesus' tomb because Jesus' body was not there. A young man by the tomb said to Mary:

Angel: Why are you crying?

Mary: They have taken Jesus away. I do not know where they have put Him.

Narrator: When Mary said this, she saw Jesus standing by her, but she did not know that it was Jesus.

Jesus: Why are you crying? Who are you looking for?

Narrator: Mary thought at first that Jesus was the gardener.

Mary: If you took Jesus away, tell me where you have put Him. I will go and get Him.

Narrator: Then Jesus said her name.

Jesus: Mary!

Narrator: Mary turned toward Jesus. She knew who it was. She said:

Mary: Teacher!

Jesus: Go tell My friends that I am going back to My Father.

Narrator: Mary went back to Jesus' friends and told them that she had seen Jesus. He was alive!

From John 20:11–18

COMING TO FAITH

What did you learn from the story of Mary Magdalene at the tomb?

On Easter we show how happy we are that Jesus is alive. He shares His new life with us. We pray and sing Alleluia.

Sing this happy Alleluia song.
(To the tune of "Skip to My Lou")

♫ Alle! Alleluia!
Alle! Alleluia!
Alle! Alleluia!
Jesus gives us new life! ♫

PRACTICING FAITH

Make an Easter Good News banner.
Share the banner with your family.
How will you celebrate the good news
of Easter at home and in your parish?

Take a few minutes to talk with the
children about ways they and their
families might use the "Faith Alive"
pages. Encourage them to share signs
of new life with their families.

FAITH ALIVE AT HOME AND IN THE PARISH

In this lesson your child learned that after Jesus died He rose to new life. It is this new life that He shares with us. We celebrate the resurrection of Jesus every Sunday.

But the high point is Easter Sunday itself. It is the day of Jesus' final victory over death and destruction—it is the feast of our Christian hope. We are assured in the resurrection of Jesus that we, too, can rise with Him to new life.

Easter, then, is a time for a renewed and living faith—a faith that reaches out to the poor, the abandoned, and the homeless, so that they may also find the hope of new life in our acts of Christian love, concern and justice.

You might ask yourself:

■ *How does the Easter message give me hope?*

■ *How can our family bring the hope of Easter to someone else? to people in our parish?*

Learn by heart
Faith Summary

- Jesus rose from the dead on Easter.
- Jesus gives us new life.

New Life

Celebrate the new life Jesus gives at Easter. Decorate the T-shirt with signs of Easter joy.

Review

Go over the *Faith Summary* together before having your child complete the *Review.* The answers for questions 1–3 appear on page 200. Use the response to number 4 to discuss your child's feelings about Jesus' new life. When the *Review* is completed, have your child put a sticker on the page.

Circle the correct word.

1. Jesus gives us new _____.

clothes   life

2. We celebrate Jesus' new life on _____.

Easter   New Year's Day

3. When Jesus' friend went to His tomb, it was _____.

closed   empty

4. How will you share with someone the good news of Easter?

FAMILY SCRIPTURE MOMENT

Gather and **Listen** to the joyful Easter story.

Very early on Sunday morning the women went to the tomb, carrying the spices they had prepared. They stood there puzzled about this [the empty tomb], when suddenly two men in bright shining clothes stood by them. Full of fear, the women bowed down to the ground, as the men said to them, "Why are you looking among the dead for one who is alive? He is not here; He has been raised. Remember what He said to you while He was in Galilee: 'The Son of Man must be handed over to sinful men, be crucified, and three days later rise to life.'"

From Luke 24:1,4–7

Share Imagine you were at the tomb on the first Easter. How might you have reacted?

Consider for family enrichment:

■ This story of the resurrection shows us the women disciples at the empty tomb. They are the first witnesses to tell of Jesus' resurrection from the dead.

■ The resurrection is the heart of the Christian faith. We, too, go forth to share this joyful message with others.

Reflect and **Decide** How will your family celebrate your Easter faith this year? Think of something very special to do together.

142

UNIT 3 • REVIEW

Jesus sends the Holy Spirit.

God the Holy Spirit helped the friends of Jesus to pray and to remember that Jesus wanted them to love others. The Holy Spirit helped them to tell everyone the good news of Jesus.

The Church begins.

The Church is Jesus Christ and His baptized friends joined together by the Holy Spirit. The Holy Spirit helps the friends of Jesus to be His Church and to live as Christians.

We celebrate Baptism.

When we are baptized, we become God's own children. We receive God's own life and love. We become part of the Church.

We celebrate Mass.

Mass is our great celebration together. We listen to God's word from the Bible. We receive the Body and Blood of Jesus in Holy Communion.

UNIT 3 ▪ TEST

Read to me

Fill in the circle beside the correct answer.

1. We belong to Jesus'___.

   ○ room   ○ Church   ○ help

2. The ___ is with us today.

   ○ friend   ○ Holy Spirit   ○ children

3. We receive ___ in Holy Communion.

   ○ Jesus   ○ water   ○ candles

4. In Baptism I became a ___ of God.

   ○ child   ○ flower   ○ book

5. Tell how you will love someone as Jesus did.

Child's name _____

Your child has just completed Unit 3. Have your child bring this paper to the catechist. It will help you and the catechist know better how to help your child grow in the faith.

____ My child needs help with the part of the Review/Summary I have underlined.
____ My child understands what has been taught in this unit.
____ I would like to speak with you. My phone number is _____.

(Signature)_____

22 Our Parish Church

Jesus, help us
to work together
as Your friends.

Our Life

Read to me
Down in the valley,
In the bottom of the sea,
Lived a crab named Charlie,
Who was cranky as can be.

Down in the valley,
In the bottom of the sea,
Lived a fish named Sharkey,
Who was friendly as can be.

Sharkey got the starfish
And some other fishy friends
To write this note to Charlie,
Which they signed and then
   did send.

"Dear Charlie, when you're lonely,
And need a friend to care,
Please come to our special place.
You're always welcome there!"

How did Sharkey help Charlie?

How do friends help you?

How do you cheer up your friends
when they are sad?

Sharing Life

Do friends need a place
to be together? Why?

Do Jesus' friends need
a special place
to be together? Why?

OUR CATHOLIC FAITH

Our Parish Belongs to All of Us

Our parish is our special place
in the Catholic Church.
We come together with other
Catholic families who live near us.

Our parish belongs to all of us.
We learn about Jesus in our parish.
We learn to live as Jesus' friends.

Our parish has a special building
called the parish church.
We are baptized there.
We celebrate the Mass there.
We pray and worship God there.

Everyone in our parish is welcome.
When visitors come, we say,
"Welcome to our parish!"

Write the name of your parish.

_____

- -

_____

The **parish** is our special place in the Catholic Church.

We All Help Our Parish

Everyone in our parish is important. We all have something special to do.

Many people make up our parish family. There are young people, old people, families, and friends.

Some people read God's word to us. Some of them give us Holy Communion.

Some people in our parish help the poor, the sick, and the lonely. Some people teach us about God.

The priest in our parish leads us as we worship God at Mass. He also helps us care for one another.

Write the name of a priest in your parish. Call him by name when you see him.

Hello, Father

_____

- -

_____

147

Coming To Faith

Tell three ways people help
one another in your parish.

Some people in our parish
are sick. They cannot go outside.
Let's help someone.
Send them a special surprise.

Trace the fish and cut it out. Color the fish.
Join it with others to make an underwater scene.
Write on your picture, "We love you!"

Ask your catechist or pastor
to bring your scene to someone
in your parish who is sick.

Practicing Faith

Name one way you would like
to help in your parish this week.

Invite one of your friends to visit your
parish church.

Talk to the children
about ways they and
their families might use
the "Faith Alive" pages.
Then pray the prayer for
the Church on page 149
as a closing faith
response.

FAITH ALIVE AT HOME AND IN THE PARISH

Parishes are joined together in a diocese under the leadership of the bishop. All the bishops, together with the pope as bishop of Rome, serve as leaders of the universal Church.

The parish is our home in the Catholic Church. It is critical that every Catholic feels a sense of welcome and belonging in his or her parish home. Whether or not children will feel that they belong to their Catholic faith as adults will depend very much on their feelings of belonging to their parish as children. You have to build up this sense of parish as home for your family and for your fellow parishioners.

You might ask yourself:

■ *In what ways does my parish welcome me and help me feel I belong? In what ways do I help others feel they belong?*

■ *In what ways can I and my family share in the liturgical and catechetical life of our parish?*

One way to help children feel the parish is their home is to have them invite friends to the parish church. You might want to do the activity below with your child.

A Family Prayer

Pray this prayer for the Church with your child.

† Jesus, bless our parish family.
Bless Your Church all over the world.
Help us to live like You.
Help us to share Your good news with everyone.

Learn by heart Faith Summary

- Our parish is our special place in the Catholic Church.
- Everyone helps in our parish.

Invite a friend to visit your parish church. Practice your invitation here. Then copy it on note paper.

Join Us

FOR:_____

DATE:_____ TIME:_____

PLACE:_____

_____

149

Review

First go over the *Faith Summary* with your child. Then have him or her complete the *Review. The answers for questions 1–3 appear on page 200.* Use the response to number 4 to discuss with your child her or his feeling of belonging in the parish.

Talk to your child about ways you can both feel more at home in your parish. When the *Review* is completed, have your child place a sticker on this page.

sticker

Circle the correct word.

1. Our parish has a special building called the parish _____.

church   altar

2. We _____ to God in our parish church.

pray   name

3. The _____ leads us as we worship God at Mass.

priest   team

4. Tell how you feel about belonging to your parish.

FAMILY SCRIPTURE MOMENT

Gather and **Listen** as a family.

An argument broke out among the disciples as to which one of them should be thought of as the greatest. Jesus said to them, "The kings of the pagans have power over their people, and the rulers claim the title 'Friends of the People.' But this is not the way it is with you; rather, the greatest among you must be like the youngest, and the leader must be like the servant. Who is greater, the one who sits down to eat or the one who serves? The one who sits down, of course. But I am among you as one who serves."

From Luke 22:24–27

Share What do we hear Jesus saying in the words, "I am among you as one who serves"? What are some ways we can serve one another?

Consider for family enrichment:

■ Luke places Jesus' teaching about greatness and service in the context of the Last Supper. The disciples of Jesus are not to lord it over others but to lovingly serve others, as He did.

■ As disciples, we are also called to serve others in the Christian community and the world, especially those most in need.

Reflect and **Decide** What does it mean to be great among those who follow Jesus? How will we show greatness in the parish this week?

23 Our Catholic Church

Our Life

Here is a poem about the wind.
Make up your own actions.

Who has seen the wind?
Neither I nor you.
But when the leaves
    hang trembling,
The wind is passing through.

Who has seen the wind?
Neither you nor I.
But when the leaves
    bow down their heads,
The wind is passing by.

Christina G. Rossetti

We do not see the wind.
How do you know that the wind is blowing?

We do not see God.
How do we know that God is with us?

Sharing Life

How does knowing that God is
with you make you feel?
Tell Him in the quiet of your heart.

Our Church Celebrates

Jesus gave His Church special signs that God is with us. They are called sacraments. In the sacraments, our Church does what Jesus did to show God's love and care for everyone.

Jesus welcomed all people into His community of friends. In the sacrament of Baptism, our Church welcomes all people into our Church community. Jesus promised to send the Holy Spirit to be our Helper. In the sacrament of Confirmation, the Holy Spirit comes to us in a special way.

Jesus fed people who were hungry. In the sacrament of Eucharist, the Church gives us Jesus Himself to be our food in Holy Communion.

Jesus forgave people their sins. In the sacrament of Reconciliation, the Church brings us God's forgiveness and mercy.

Catholics all over the world celebrate the sacraments. When we celebrate the sacraments, we worship God together.

To **worship** is to give honor and praise to God.

Our Church Prays

Our Church also worships God
when we pray together or alone.
Jesus wants His friends to pray.
He tells us, "Pray always."

From Luke 21:36

Sometimes we pray in our own words.
Sometimes we sing our prayers.
Sometimes we pray the prayer
Jesus taught us, the Our Father.

Catholics also pray to Mary,
the mother of Jesus.
We ask Mary to pray to God for us.
We say the Hail Mary.

✝ Hail Mary, full of grace,
the Lord is with you;
blessed are you among women,
and blessed is the fruit
of your womb, Jesus.

Holy Mary, Mother of God,
pray for us sinners
now and at the hour of our death.
Amen.

When we celebrate and pray, we live
as Jesus' friends.

153

COMING TO FAITH

Make up a thank-you prayer for each of the sacraments.

Baptism   Confirmation

Eucharist   Reconciliation

Sing these words after each prayer.
(To the tune of "Michael, Row the Boat")

♫ Let us pray and celebrate, Alleluia,
Gifts and signs of God's great love,
Alleluia. ♫

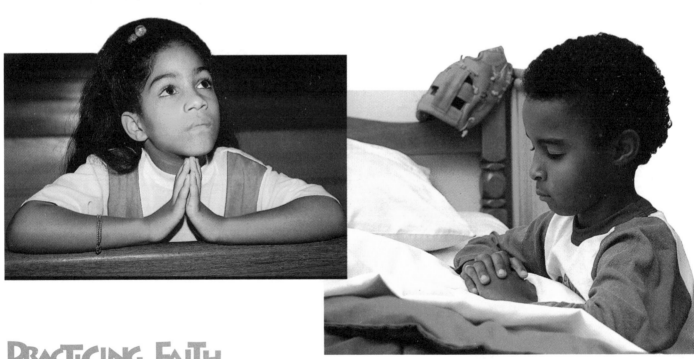

PRACTICING FAITH

Circle ways that you will celebrate and pray. Tell about them.

Gather in a circle and hold hands. Pray the Hail Mary together.

154

Take a few minutes to talk with the children about ways they and their families might use the "Faith Alive" pages. Encourage them to pray the Hail Mary with someone at home each night this week.

FAITH ALIVE AT HOME AND IN THE PARISH

When we take part often, knowingly, and lovingly in the Church's life of prayer and worship, we experience ourselves as a priestly people. It is an aspect of our baptismal commitment to "proclaim the wonderful acts of God, who called us out of darkness into God's own marvelous light" (from 1 Peter 2:9).

Celebrating the sacraments and praying often as a family are wonderful ways to help our children grow strong in their Christian faith and in their love of God.

You might ask yourself:

■ *What sacraments and other Church celebrations help me most in my daily life?*

■ *When will I take time for personal prayer this week?*

Have your child say the Hail Mary slowly with you. Talk about what it means to both of you.

Reflective Prayer

Before your child goes to bed, you might gently ask one or two questions like these: Did you help anyone today? Did you play fairly? Did you try to do your best work in school? Then together thank God for the times your child did one of these things.

Learn by heart **Faith Summary**

- Catholics celebrate the sacraments.
- Catholics pray to God.

Add some of your favorite things to the card.

Hail Mary, full of grace, The Lord is with you.

Hello,

_____.
(your name)
I am a child of God.
The Lord is with me.

Pray and **remember.**

Review

First go over the *Faith Summary* with your child. Then have him or her complete the *Review*. The answers for questions 1–3 appear on page 200. The response to number 4 will help you see whether your child feels comfortable with praying and is developing the habit of praying often. When the *Review* is completed, have your child place a sticker on this page.

Circle the correct word.

1. The prayer that Jesus taught us is the _____.

Our Father   Bible

2. To worship is to give honor and praise to _____.

others   God

3. Catholics celebrate the _____.

sacraments   candles

4. What is your favorite prayer?

When do you pray this prayer?

FAMILY SCRIPTURE MOMENT

Gather and tell about some of the "mighty" things God has done for you. Then **Listen** to Mary's song of praise.

My heart praises the Lord;
    my soul is glad because of
        God my Savior,
    for He has remembered me,
        His lowly servant!
From now on all people will
        call me happy,
    because of the great things
        the mighty God has done for me.

Luke 1:46–49

Share For us, what does it mean to be blessed?

Consider for family enrichment:

■ These are the first lines of Mary's canticle, the Magnificat. She shared this song of praise with Elizabeth, expressing her joy in being chosen by God as the mother of His own Son.

■ Mary's canticle is part of the daily Evening Prayer of the Church. It reminds us that God works through the "little ones" to accomplish great works of love, justice, and peace.

Reflect and **Decide** Pray the Magnificat together. Invite each person to choose one way to be God's faithful servant this week.

Jesus, help us
to be fair
to everyone.

OUR LIFE

Look at each picture.
Tell what is happening.

Which children are being fair?
Which child is being unfair?

Have you ever been treated unfairly?
How did you feel?

Do you ever treat others unfairly?
How?

SHARING LIFE

What does it mean to be unfair to someone?

Why are we sometimes unfair to others?

Why do you think Jesus wants us to be fair
to everyone?

Our Catholic Faith

The Church Helps People

The Catholic Church helps people by teaching us how to be fair. The Church helps us to know what Jesus taught.

Here is a story Jesus told about being fair.

Read to me from the Bible

Once there was a servant who owed the king a lot of money. He could not pay what he owed. He begged the king, "Please give me more time to pay what I owe you." The king felt sorry for his servant. He said, "You do not have to pay me back any money."

The servant was very happy. Then he went to see a man who owed him a little money. The man begged, "Please give me more time to pay what I owe you." The servant said, "No! You must pay me now!"

The king was very angry at the way his servant treated the man. He said, "You should have been fair to the man, just as I was fair to you."

From Matthew 18:22–34

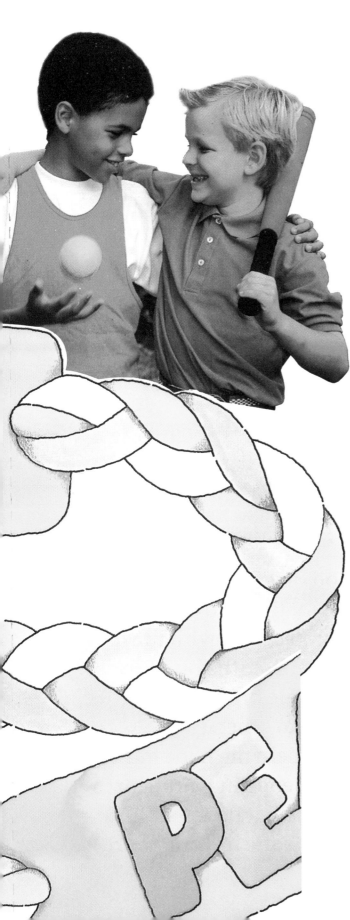

What do you learn from this story?

Being fair means treating people the way we want them to treat us. It also means caring for people who need our help, especially the poor.

Jesus teaches us that it does not matter how young or old a person is. It does not matter what color skin a person has. God wants us to be fair to everyone.

When we are fair, we show people that God loves everyone.
When we are fair to one another, we help to make peace.

Peace means not fighting.
Peace means being quiet inside ourselves.

Jesus gives us His gift of peace.
Jesus said,
"My peace is My gift to you."

From John 14:27

Coming To Faith

Be a peace partner!
Pretend you are Jesus.
How can you help the
children in each picture
act fairly and make peace?

What would Jesus say?

What would Jesus do?

Take a few minutes to talk to the
children about ways they and their
families might use the "Faith Alive"
pages. Encourage them to talk with
someone at home about ways they
will try to be fair to others this week.

Practicing Faith

Jesus wants us to be fair
and to keep peace in our hearts.

Be still. Pray slowly.

✝ Jesus, You give me peace.
(Breathe in. Breathe out.)
May Your peace be with me always.
(Breathe in. Breathe out.)
Jesus, help me bring
Your peace to others.
This week, help me to be fair to . . .
(Name someone in your heart.)
Help me to be at peace with . . .
(Name someone in your heart.)

FAITH ALIVE AT HOME AND IN THE PARISH

The Church's social teaching on justice and peace is soundly rooted in the Old and New Testaments. That the covenant demands justice is a constant theme of the Hebrew prophets.

From the proclamation of Jesus' birth to His farewell at the Last Supper, the life of Christ preaches justice and peace to all people. The Catholic Church clearly teaches that our Christian faith gives us serious social responsibilities. All of us are called to work for God's kingdom of justice and peace in the world.

Children need to be given opportunities to practice fairness and forgiveness in their daily lives. In the family the habits of justice, mercy, and peace must be sown if children are to grow to be just and merciful adults.

You might ask yourself:

■ *How do we as a family respond to the Church's call to be people of justice, mercy, and peace?*

■ *What will we do this week to make the first move toward peace with someone or some group?*

To help your child to be a peaceful person, pray with him or her in the way described below.

Talk About Fairness

Help your child in his or her daily life to notice opportunities for practicing fairness with others. Also encourage your child to talk with Jesus about hurts and worries.

Learn by heart ## Faith Summary

- Catholics try to treat others fairly and live in peace.
- Jesus wants us to be peacemakers.

Finding Peace

Close your eyes. Breathe in and out slowly. Imagine you are a boat, sailing in the wind. Pray this prayer.

Peace to you.
Peace to me.
Peace within our family.

Review
First go over the *Faith Summary* with your child. Then have him or her complete the *Review*. The answers for questions 1–3 appear on page 200. The response to number 4 will give you the chance to talk about the times when she or he finds it hard to be fair. When the *Review* is completed, have your child place a sticker on this page.

sticker

Circle the correct word.

1. Jesus gave the gift of _____ to us.

peace   sadness

2. When we are fair to one another, we can live in _____.

sadness   peace

3. Being fair is treating people the way we _____.

feel like treating them   want them to treat us

4. I will try to be fair _____.

sometimes   always

FAMILY SCRIPTURE MOMENT

Gather and **Listen** as Jesus speaks to us.

A healthy tree does not bear bad fruit, nor does a poor tree bear good fruit. Every tree is known by the fruit it bears; you do not pick figs from thorn bushes or gather grapes from bramble bushes. A good person brings good out of the treasure of good things in the heart. For the mouth speaks what the heart is full of.

From Luke 6:43–45

Share What evidence, or "fruit," do we produce to show we are Christians?

Consider for family enrichment:

■ Jesus used the example of a fig tree because figs were an important source of energy and nutrition to the people of His country. Figs were eaten year-round.

■ Our good words and deeds of Christian service must come from our hearts.

Reflect and ask, "What is the good fruit that I want to bring forth as a Christian?"

Decide How will our mouths speak what our hearts are full of to the sick or the needy this week?

25 God Forgives Us

OUR LIFE

Read to me
I was very angry.
My face turned red,
When I heard
What my sister said.

She started to fight
In the middle of the game.
I got upset,
And called a name.

Mom told us both
To forgive and forget,
But I don't think
We can do that yet.

Has something like this
Ever happened to you?
Tell about it.
What did you do?

SHARING LIFE

Tell how you feel when
you forgive someone.

Tell how you feel when
someone forgives you.

Does God want us to forgive
other people? Why?

Why do we sometimes need
to ask God to forgive us?

We Show We Are Sorry

We are God's children. We know that God wants us to love Him, love others, and love ourselves.

But sometimes we do not live as God's children. We do not do what God wants. We do things we know we should not do. We sin.

We need to show others we are sorry if we have hurt them. There are lots of ways to tell others, "I am sorry."

We can give a hug.
We can shake hands.
We can say what is in our hearts.

When we sin we need to tell God that we are sorry.

God Forgives Us

God always loves us, no matter what we do. He always forgives us if we are sorry. In the Bible Jesus told this story to teach us that God always forgives.

Read to me from the Bible

Once there was a young man who decided to take his money and leave his father's home. When all his money was gone, all his friends left him. He had no place to stay and nothing to eat. He knew he had done wrong. He decided to go back home and tell his father how sorry he was.

His father was so happy to see him! He forgave his son and had a party to welcome him home.
From Luke 15:11–24

In the Catholic Church we have a special way to celebrate that God forgives us. It is called the sacrament of Reconciliation.

How wonderful it is to know that God forgives us and that His life of grace is in us.

COMING TO FAITH

Tell the Bible story
about the son who left home.
Follow the path that leads him
back home to his father.
Tell what the father said
when he saw his son.

Does God always forgive us
when we are sorry?
Why?

PRACTICING FAITH

Do you need to ask someone to forgive
you? What will you say?

Is there someone you would like to
forgive? What will you say?

Turn to page 76. Find the words in the
Our Father that tell us about forgiveness.
Pray the Our Father together.

166

Take a few minutes to talk with the
children about ways they and their
families might share the "Faith Alive"
pages. Encourage them to pray the
Our Father with someone at home
and to talk about what it means to say
"Forgive us our trespasses."

FAITH ALIVE AT HOME AND IN THE PARISH

In this lesson your child has been given a basic understanding that in the sacrament of Reconciliation the Church continues Jesus' ministry of forgiving sinners.

Reconciliation restores us to God's grace and strengthens our friendship with Him. Such forgiveness means not just telling God we are sorry, but also seeking ways of repairing any harm done to those we have hurt. This lesson also helps your child understand the need for each of us to forgive others.

You and your family must also help your child begin to understand what it means to say both "I am sorry" and "I forgive you." This means showing *how* you are sorry and *how* you forgive. Think of ways you can model both to your child this week.

Talk with your child about how he or she feels when forgiving or when being forgiven. Then ask your child to complete the activity below.

Sharing Prayers
Go over this part of the Our Father with your child:

✝ "Forgive us our trespasses as we forgive those who trespass against us."

Point out the importance of forgiving others as we wish God to forgive us.

Learn by heart ## Faith Summary

- God always forgives us if we are sorry.
- The Church forgives in God's name.

Circle how you feel when you forgive or when you are forgiven. Act it out.

167

Review
First go over the *Faith Summary* with your child. Then have him or her complete the *Review*. The answers for questions 1–3 appear on page 200. The response to number 4 will help you discuss

with your child the habit of asking forgiveness. When the *Review* is completed have your child place a sticker on this page.

Circle the correct word.

1. God forgives us when we are _____.

sorry   happy

2. _____ brings us God's forgiveness.

John   Jesus

3. God will _____ love us.

always   sometimes

4. Tell how you feel when you have been forgiven.

FAMILY SCRIPTURE MOMENT

Gather and ask: How important is forgiveness in everyday living? Then **Listen** to the words of Jesus in this story.

Then Jesus said to the woman, "Your sins are forgiven." The others sitting at the table began to say to themselves, "Who is this, who even forgives sins?" But Jesus said to the woman, "Your faith has saved you; go in peace."
Luke 7:48–50

Share Invite family members to share what they heard in this reading.

Consider for family enrichment:
■ This reading is an excerpt from a story about a

sinful woman who humbly washed Jesus' feet and anointed His head when He was at the home of Simon the Pharisee. Because she showed such great love for Jesus, He forgave all her sins. We, too, receive God's forgiveness in a special way in the sacrament of Reconciliation.

■ When we forgive others, we reflect the mercy and compassion of God.

Reflect How and for what will we try to show forgiveness in our family?

Decide Exchange some sign of peace and forgiveness with one another.

26 Living With God Forever

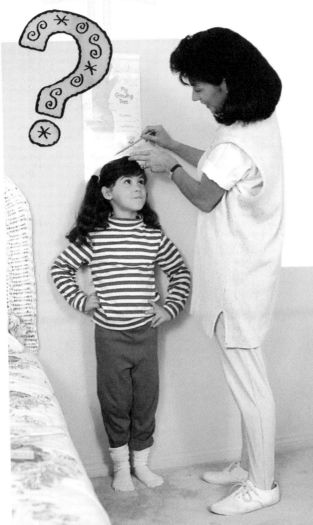

Our Life

Imagine you are in second grade.
Ask yourself these questions.

Will I look the same as I do today?
Will I be taller than I am now?
Will I have the same number of teeth?
Will I be in the same classroom?
Will I have the same teacher?
Will I like to do the same things?

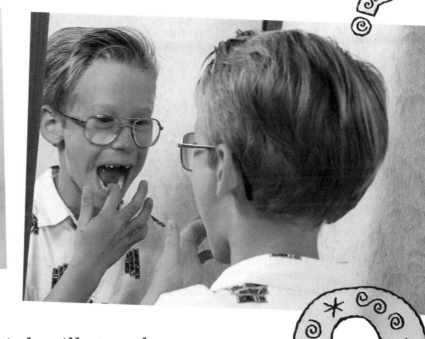

Sharing Life

What do you think will stay the same
about you? Why?

What do you think will be different?
Why?

Does anything stay the same forever?

What do you think lasts forever?

169

We Can Be with God Forever

This Bible story shows us how much Jesus loves us and wants us to be with God forever.

Read to me from the Bible

One day some people brought
their children to see Jesus.
The friends of Jesus told them
to go away and not to bother Jesus.

Jesus was angry at this.
He said to His friends,
"Let the children come to Me.
The kingdom of God belongs to them."

Then Jesus took the children
in His arms and blessed them.
From Mark 10:13–16

We are God's own children and friends of Jesus. If we live as children of God, as Jesus showed us, we will be happy with God forever in heaven.

Here is some of the good news we learned this year. Remembering these things will help us live as children of God and friends of Jesus.

Good News

- Jesus showed us how to love God, one another, and ourselves.

- Jesus taught us how to be fair and to live in peace.

- Jesus taught us to help people in need.

- God made us and loves us.

- God's greatest gift is Jesus, the Son of God.

- We try to follow Jesus.

- Jesus died and rose to new life for us.

- Jesus gave us the Church.

- We became members of the Church at Baptism.

- The Holy Spirit helps us to live as children of God.

- The Catholic Church is our special home in the Christian family.

- God's love for us will never end.

COMING TO FAITH

Imagine you are sitting with Jesus.
Talk to Him about what
you have learned.
Tell Him how you will try
to live as a child of God.

I will pray

I will worship God at Mass

I will be kind

I will be fair

PRACTICING FAITH

Mark the pennants to tell
what you will do this summer
to show that you are God's child.

Pray,
† Dear Jesus, help us stay close to you.
Help us to grow as God's children
this summer.

Take a few minutes to talk to the
children about ways they and their
families might use the "Faith Alive"
pages. Encourage them to work with
someone at home to create a weekly
chart as a reminder to grow as God's
child during the summer.

Your child has now completed *Coming to God,* the first grade book about our Catholic faith. Your family is to be congratulated for its continued interest and support in your child's growth in faith. Your interest need not stop here but should continue through the coming weeks with experiences of prayer and good works. Living as friends of Jesus is a lifetime vocation.

Recall with your child some of the most important truths learned this year. Discuss the importance of God's word and presence in your family's life. You may wish to end by acting out the poem adapted from Ephesians 3:17.

With your child make a weekly chart to show how he or she can live as a child of God.

Remembering Baptism

Discuss with your child God's unending love. Light a candle and pray:

† "This is the light of Christ. May it always burn brightly in your heart and lead you to be with God forever and ever."

Wider than the widest sea

Taller than the tallest tree

Deep as the deepest lake can be—

God's Love for Me
Move your arms
to help you remember
what God's love is like.

 **Faith Summary**

- Jesus wants us to be with Him forever.
- God's love will never end.

That is God's great love for me!

sticker

Circle the correct word.

1. God will stay with me _____.

    a day   forever

2. God's _____ will last forever.

    love   fear

3. Jesus blessed the _____.

    day   children

4. Tell one thing you will do to show you are God's child.

FAMILY SCRIPTURE MOMENT

Gather and ask: What do you think Jesus loves so much about children? Then **Listen** to our final reading from Luke's gospel.

An argument broke out among the disciples as to which one of them was the greatest. Jesus knew what they were thinking, so He took a child, stood the child by His side, and said to them, "Whoever welcomes this child in My name, welcomes Me; and whoever welcomes Me, also welcomes the One who sent Me. For the one who is least among you is the greatest."
From Luke 9:46–49

Share In what ways are we, no matter how old we get, to remain like children?

Consider for family enrichment:

■ Jesus understands that His disciples will always be tempted to be "big and important," to be "the greatest" in other people's eyes. So He tells them that real greatness is to be childlike before God.

■ By our Baptism we are God's children, called to welcome and serve, as Jesus did.

Reflect Reread Luke 9:46–49. What will we remember best about this reading?

Decide Close with a simple fun family celebration that includes a prayer of thanksgiving to God.

Jesus, give
us peace
in our hearts.

Let us celebrate God's gifts
of forgiveness and peace.
Make a peace pinwheel.

Be still.
Imagine you are the
pinwheel turning.
Pray slowly.

✝ God's peace . . .
God's peace be in me . . .
God's peace be with us all . . .

175

✝ God, may this story help us to remember that You will always love us and are always ready to forgive us. Help us always be ready to forgive one another.

Reader: Once there was a young man who decided to take his father's money and leave his father's home. He went far away, and spent his money on things that were not good for him. When all his money was gone, he had no place to stay and nothing to eat. He knew he had been wrong. He decided to go back home and tell his father how sorry he was.

His father was very happy to see his son once more. He forgave his son and had a party to welcome him home.

From Luke 15:11–24

Leader: Let us use this picture to help us imagine the story Jesus told us about the forgiving father. Think about these questions in your heart:

- How do you think the son feels?
- How do you think the father feels?
- How do you feel when someone who loves you forgives you?

Leader: Now we will say "We are sorry in our hearts." We will ask Jesus to forgive us. We will forgive one another.

Child 1: For the times that we fought with a brother, a sister, or a friend,
All: Jesus, we are sorry.

Child 2: For the times we took something from our friends,
All: Jesus, we are sorry.

Child 3: For the times we disobeyed our parents and did not show respect to older people,
All: Jesus, we are sorry.

Child 4: For the times we did not do the good things we could have done,
All: Jesus, we are sorry.

Child 5: For all the times we have been good and tried to do what You want us to do,
All: Thank You, Jesus!

Turn your pinwheels slowly as you
sing the following song prayer.
(To the tune of "Kumbaya")

♫ Give us peace, Jesus, in our hearts. (3x)
O Jesus, give us peace.

Give us peace, Jesus, in our homes. (3x)
O Jesus, give us peace.

Give us peace, Jesus, with our friends. (3x)
O Jesus, give us peace.

Give us peace, Jesus, in our Church. (3x)
O Jesus, give us peace. ♫

Now give one another a sign of peace.

SUMMARY 2 • REVIEW

Jesus Christ sends the Holy Spirit.
The Holy Spirit helps the friends of Jesus. The Holy Spirit helps them to be peacemakers.

The Holy Spirit comes to us when we are baptized.

When we are baptized, we become part of the Church.

We receive God's own life and love.

We belong to the Catholic Church.
Everyone is welcome in our Church. The Church helps us to be holy people.

We celebrate the sacraments and try to live fairly and to be peacemakers.

If we live as children of God, as Jesus showed us, we will be happy with God forever in heaven.

SUMMARY 2 • TEST

Read to me

Fill in the circle next to each correct answer.

1. The Holy Spirit helps ____.

   ⭕ me   ⭕ animals   ⭕ plants

2. We are part of the ____.

   ⭕ circus   ⭕ sea   ⭕ Church

3. The ____ is the good news of Jesus.

   ⭕ singing   ⭕ Gospel   ⭕ loving

4. Jesus' Church is for ____.

   ⭕ no one   ⭕ someone   ⭕ everyone

5. Tell about one way you will be fair to someone.

The Mass ends.

The priest blesses us.
Then the priest or deacon says,

"Go in peace to love and serve
the Lord."

We answer,
"Thanks be to God."

16

My
Mass
Book

Fold on this line.

‑‑‑‑‑‑‑‑‑‑‑‑‑‑✂‑‑‑‑‑‑‑‑‑‑ Cut on this line. ‑‑‑‑‑‑‑‑‑‑‑‑‑‑‑‑‑‑‑‑‑‑‑‑‑‑‑‑

Jesus gives us the gift
of Himself in Holy Communion.

14

We ask God to forgive us.

"Lord, have mercy.
Christ, have mercy.
Lord, have mercy."

After a prayer, we
sit and get ready to
hear God's word.

3

We gather as a parish family.
We stand and pray.

† In the name of the Father,
and of the Son,
and of the Holy Spirit.
We answer,
"Amen."

Cut on this line.

Fold on this line.

Communion time is a
wonderful time for us
to pray.

You can say,
† "Jesus, come and live
in my heart."

Liturgy of the Word

We listen to God's word.
The reader says,
"The word of the Lord."

We answer,
"Thanks be
to God."

We share the gift of peace.
We say,
"Peace be with you."

We stand and pray the prayer
Jesus taught us.

† "Our Father, who art in heaven,
hallowed be thy name;
thy kingdom come;
thy will be done on earth
as it is in heaven.
Give us this day our daily bread;
and forgive us our trespasses
as we forgive those
who trespass against us;
and lead us not into temptation,
but deliver us from evil."

Cut on this line.

"This is the cup of my blood."

Fold on this line.

We stand for the gospel.
The priest or deacon says,
"The Lord be with you."

We answer,
"And also with you."

After the gospel, the priest or
deacon says,
"The gospel of the Lord."

We say,
"Praise to you, Lord Jesus Christ."

The priest invites us to pray.
He says,
"Lift up your hearts."

We answer,
"We lift them up to the Lord."

Liturgy of the Eucharist

Our gifts of bread and wine are carried to the altar.

The priest prepares our gifts to be offered to God.

Cut on this line.

"Do this in memory of me."

We remember what Jesus said and did at the Last Supper.

We pray,
"Holy,
   holy,
      holy
Lord, God of power and might...."

The priest does what Jesus did at the Last Supper and says,

"This is my body which will be given up for you."

My Catholic Faith Book

For the Family

As your child's first grade experience ends, we celebrate with you the ways in which your child has grown as a child of God. You have guided your child's growth in the wisdom of Christian faith, including a love for Scripture. During this year, your child has learned and experienced some very important truths of our faith as they are contained in the *Catechism of the Catholic Church*. For example:

• Creed: God's greatest gift is Jesus Christ, the Son of God. We are members of God's family, the Church. The Holy Spirit helps us to live as children of God.

• Sacraments: We become members of the Church at Baptism. We thank Jesus at Mass for the gift of Himself in the Eucharist. In the sacrament of Reconciliation, we celebrate God's forgiveness. We are strengthened by the Holy Spirit at Confirmation.

• Morality: We try to follow Jesus. We try to love God, one another, and ourselves. We try to be fair and to live in peace.

• Prayer: We listen to God's word in the Bible. We talk to God in our own words. We pray the Our Father, the Hail Mary, and the Sign of the Cross.

Continue to encourage your child to grow in faith by going to Mass together, singing the faith songs, reading Bible stories about God's love for us, and praying together.

Family Prayer

Dear God,
Help our family to continue to grow in faith each day. God, help us as we grow more like Jesus Christ, Your Son. Amen.

This is what we believe…

God made the world and all people.
Everything God made is good.
We are made by God who loves us.

He knows and loves and creates all things.

God made us to know and love
and make things, too.

C R E E D

There is only one God.

There are three Persons in one God:
God the Father, God the Son, and
God the Holy Spirit.

We call the three Persons in God
the Blessed Trinity.
God's love for us will never end.

This is how we pray…

We can pray anywhere or anytime
by ourselves or with others.

We listen to God's word in the Bible.

P R A Y E R

We talk to God in our own words
or say special prayers we have
learned, the Sign of the Cross,
the Our Father, and the Hail Mary.

We begin to learn the Apostles' Creed.

We praise , thank ,
and ask God for help.

We tell God we are sorry
if we have hurt Him
or other people.

Jesus is God's greatest gift to us. Jesus is God's own Son. He shows us how much God loves us.

Jesus gave us the Law of Love. He told us to love God, others, and ourselves.

Jesus died on Good Friday and rose from the dead on Easter Sunday. He is alive and with us today. Jesus gives us new life.

Jesus gave us the Church.

This is how we live...

M We try to follow Jesus.

O We try to follow the Law of Love.

R We love God, others, and ourselves.

A We care for God's world.

L We care for all people.

I We care especially for the poor and needy.

T We try to live fairly.

Y We try to be peacemakers.

The Church is the community of Jesus' baptized friends.

We are joined together by the Holy Spirit. The Holy Spirit helps the friends of Jesus to be His Church.

We became members of the Church at Baptism. We are Catholic Christians.

At Baptism, we receive God's own life and love. We call this grace.

The Catholic Church is all over the world.

The Holy Spirit helps us live as children of God.

We can live forever in heaven with God.

This is how we celebrate…

We celebrate the sacrament of Baptism. When we are baptized, we receive God's own life and love.

In the sacrament of Confirmation we receive the gift of the Holy Spirit in a special way.

We celebrate the Mass. We hear God's word and share the Body and Blood of Christ.

We celebrate the sacrament of Eucharist at Mass. We share Jesus' gift of Himself in Holy Communion.

We celebrate the sacrament of Reconciliation. We tell God we are sorry and we celebrate that God is always ready to forgive us.

S
A
C
R
A
M
E
N
T
S

Morning Offering

My God, I offer you today
all I think and do and say,
uniting it with what was done
on earth, by Jesus Christ,
your Son.

Evening Prayer

Dear God, before I sleep
I want to thank you
for this day so full of
your kindness and your joy.
I close my eyes to rest
safe in your loving care.

My
Prayer
Screen

A Listening Prayer

God, open our ears
and hearts to listen
to your word.

Prayers from the Bible

God,
teach me to do
what you want.
Please show me
the way.

From Psalm 27:11

God,
I am always
in your care.

From Psalm 31:15

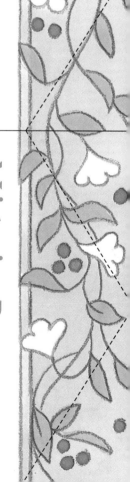

Grace Before Meals

Bless us, O Lord,

and these your gifts,

which we are about to receive

from your bounty,

through Christ our Lord.

Amen.

Grace After Meals

We give you thanks,

almighty God,

for these and all your gifts

which we have received

through Christ our Lord.

Amen.

FOLD

GLUE

GLUE

FOLD

Prayer of Quiet

Sit in a comfortable position.

Relax by breathing in and out.

Shut out all the sights

and sounds.

Each time you breathe in

and out, say the name "Jesus."

Prayer for Peace

Give us peace, Jesus,
in our hearts.

Give us peace, Jesus,
in our homes.

Give us peace, Jesus,
with our friends.

Give us peace, Jesus,
in our Church.

O, Jesus, give us peace.

Family Prayer

Come, Holy Spirit,
fill our hearts
with love.

Holy Family,
help our family
to be a
holy family, too.

A Family Blessing

May God bless us and
take care of us.
May God be kind to us.
May God look on us
with favor.
May God give us peace,
every season, every year.

From Numbers 6:24–26

FOLD

GLUE

back of screen 2

GLUE

FOLD

Prayers for Church Seasons

Advent
Come, Lord Jesus.

Christmas
Jesus, we welcome you
into our hearts.

Lent
Jesus, help me spend
quiet time with you.

Easter
Alleluia, Jesus!
We have good news
to tell.

Ordinary Time
Jesus, may our friendship
with you keep on growing.

Hail Mary

Hail Mary, full of grace,
the Lord is with you;
blessed are you
among women,
and blessed is the fruit
of your womb, Jesus.
Holy Mary, Mother of God,
pray for us sinners
now and at the hour
of our death.
Amen.

I Believe

I believe in God,
the Father almighty,
creator of heaven and earth.

The rest of the Apostles' Creed
will be taught in Grades 2 and 3.

— FOLD —

Sign of the Cross

In the name of the Father,
and of the Son,
and of the Holy Spirit.
Amen.

Our Father

Our Father, who art in heaven,
hallowed be thy name;
thy kingdom come;
thy will be done on earth
as it is in heaven.
Give us this day our daily bread
and forgive us our trespasses
as we forgive those
who trespass against us;
and lead us not into temptation
but deliver us from evil.
Amen.

— FOLD —

Glory to the Father

Glory to the Father,
and to the Son,
and to the Holy Spirit
as it was in the beginning,
is now, and will be for ever.
Amen.

A Vocation Prayer

God, I know you will
call me for special work
in my life. Help me
to follow Jesus each day
and be ready to answer
your call.

We honor Mary, the mother of Jesus, God's own Son.

We use statues and pictures to help us remember:
- Mary cared for Jesus.
- She is our mother, too.

Mary's special month is May.

- - - - ✂ -

Cut on this line.

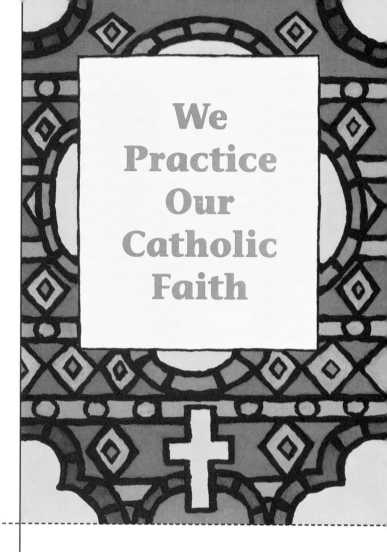

We Practice Our Catholic Faith

We pray to God at home by ourselves or with our families.
We pray to God in church with our parish family.

Fold on this line.

We are baptized.
We are God's children.
We use holy water as a sign of our Baptism.

We often begin our prayers
with the sign of the cross.
Bless yourself by making
the sign of the cross
with your right hand.

Fold on this line.

We celebrate special days
called holy days.

- The Immaculate Conception
  (December 8)

- Christmas (December 25)

- Mary, Mother of God (January 1)

- Ascension Thursday
  (40 days after Easter)

- Assumption of Mary (August 15)

- All Saints Day (November 1)

Cut on this line.

Mass is our great celebration
together.
We take part in the
Mass on Sunday
or on Saturday
evening.

We show respect and love
for God in church.
Genuflect by bending
your right knee to the floor.

GLOSSARY

Advent (page 88)
The name Christians give to our waiting time before we celebrate Jesus' birth at Christmas. We continue to wait until Jesus comes again.

Baptism (page 115)
The sacrament that gives us God's own life and love. We become God's children and belong to the Church.

Bible (page 44)
The book that tells God's story.

Blessed Trinity (page 33)
The three Persons in one God: the Father, the Son, and the Holy Spirit.

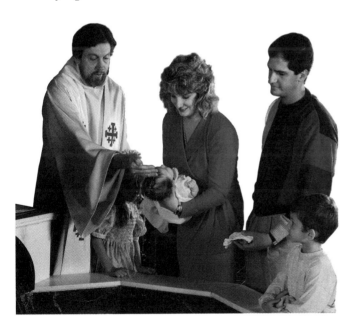

Catholic Church (page 109)
The baptized followers of Jesus who are joined together by the Holy Spirit under the leadership of the pope and bishops.

Christians (page 108)
Followers of Jesus Christ.

Christmas Day (page 58)
The day we celebrate the birth of Jesus.

Confirmation (page 152)
The sacrament in which the Holy Spirit comes to us in a special way.

Creation (page 15)
Everything made by God.

Easter Sunday (page 83)
The day Jesus rose from the dead.

Eucharist (page 152)
The sacrament in which we receive the Body and Blood of Christ.

Good Friday (page 83)
The day Jesus died on the cross for all people.

Gospel (page 126)
The good news that God loves us and gives us Jesus Christ, the Son of God.

Grace (page 27)
God's own life and love in us.

Holy Communion (page 83)
The Body and Blood of Christ.

Holy Family (page 59)
The family of Jesus, Mary, and Joseph.

Holy Spirit (page 103)
The third Person of the Blessed Trinity, the Helper sent to us by Jesus.

Jesus Christ (page 58)
The Son of God and the Son of Mary.

Last Supper (page 82)
The last meal Jesus had with His friends before He died. At this meal, Jesus gave us the gift of the Eucharist.

Law of Love (page 77)
Jesus teaches us to love God and others as we love ourselves.

Lent (page 132)
Lent is the special time before Easter.
We pray and try to grow as followers
of Jesus.

Mary (page 58)
Mary is the mother of Jesus, God's own
Son. Mary is our mother too.

Mass (page 121)
The special celebration in which
we hear God's word, remember Jesus
dying and rising, and share
the Body and Blood of Christ.

Parish (page 146)
The special place where Jesus'
friends come together to pray.

Pope (page 109)
The pope is the leader of the
Catholic Church.

Prayer (page 71)
Talking and listening to God.

Reconciliation (page 152)
The sacrament in which
the Church brings us God's
forgiveness and mercy.

Sacraments (page 152)
Signs through which Jesus shares
God's own life and love with us.

Saints (page 50)
People who loved God very much, and
who are now happy with God forever
in heaven.

Sin (page 164)
The act of freely choosing to do
what we know to be wrong. We
disobey God's law on purpose.

Worship (page 153)
Giving honor and praise to God.

Answers for Reviews

Lesson 1 (pg. 18): **1.** yes **2.** no **3.** no **4.** yes
Lesson 2 (pg. 24): **1.** yes **2.** no **3.** yes **4.** no
Lesson 3 (pg. 30): **1.** yes **2.** yes **3.** no **4.** yes
Lesson 4 (pg. 36): **1.** yes **2.** yes **3.** no **4.** yes
Lesson 5 (pg. 42): **1.** yes **2.** yes **3.** yes
Lesson 6 (pg. 48): **1.** listen **2.** love **3.** Jesus Christ
Lesson 7 (pg. 54): **1.** All Saints **2.** Saints **3.** heaven
Unit 1 (pg. 56): **1.** yes **2.** yes **3.** yes **4.** no
Lesson 8 (pg. 62): **1.** Jesus **2.** Christmas **3.** Mary
Lesson 9 (pg. 68): **1.** Son **2.** love **3.** Jesus
Lesson 10 (pg. 74): **1.** healed **2.** pray **3.** friend
Lesson 11 (pg. 80): **1.** God **2.** Our Father **3.** love
Lesson 12 (pg. 86): **1.** Last Supper **2.** Jesus **3.** died
Lesson 13 (pg. 92): **1.** yes **2.** no **3.** yes
Lesson 14 (pg. 98): **1.** no **2.** yes **3.** yes

Summary 1 (pg. 100): **1.** promises **2.** Jesus **3.** Bible **4.** human **5.** three **6.** grace
Lesson 15 (pg. 106): **1.** Christians **2.** be peacemakers **3.** Christian
Lesson 16 (pg. 112): **1.** pope **2.** Church **3.** everyone
Lesson 17 (pg. 118): **1.** Baptism **2.** water **3.** Jesus **4.** life
Lesson 18 (pg. 124): **1.** the Mass **2.** altar **3.** priest
Lesson 19 (pg. 130): **1.** gospel **2.** Creed **3.** Jesus
Lesson 20 (pg. 136): **1.** love **2.** Lent **3.** pray
Lesson 21 (pg. 142): **1.** life **2.** Easter **3.** empty
Unit 3 (pg. 144): **1.** Church **2.** Holy Spirit **3.** Jesus **4.** child
Lesson 22 (pg. 150): **1.** church **2.** pray **3.** priest
Lesson 23 (pg. 156): **1.** Our Father **2.** God **3.** sacraments
Lesson 24 (pg. 162): **1.** peace **2.** peace **3.** want them to treat us **4.** always
Lesson 25 (pg. 168): **1.** sorry **2.** Jesus **3.** always
Lesson 26 (pg. 174): **1.** forever **2.** love **3.** children
Summary 2 (pg. 180): **1.** me **2.** Church **3.** Gospel **4.** everyone

Acknowledgments

Grateful acknowledgment is due the following for their work on the *Coming to Faith* Program:

Mary Ann Trevaskiss, Project Editor
Joanna Dailey, Editor
Tresse De Lorenzo, Manager: Production/Art
Joe Svadlenka, Art Director
Eileen Elterman, Designer

Excerpts from *Good News Bible*,
copyright © American Bible Society 1966, 1971, 1976, 1979.

Excerpts from the English translation of *Rite of Baptism for Children* © 1969, International Committee on English in the Liturgy, Inc. (ICEL); excerpts from the English translation of *The Roman Missal* © 1973, ICEL. All rights reserved.

English translation of the Lord's Prayer and the Gloria Patri by the International Consultation on English Texts.

Photo Research
Jim Saylor

Cover Photos

Peter Brandt : *background and nature insets.*
Myrleen Cate : *top right insets.*
CNS/ CROSIERS : *bottom left insets.*

Photo Credits

J. Angauer/ MARYKNOLL : 114.
Diane Ali : 44, 139 *bottom left.*
Jeffrey Aranita : 113.
Eric Bean : 121 *background.*
James Carroll : 193 *bottom right,* 194 *bottom right.*
CNS/ CROSIERS : 109 *left.*
CROSIERS/ Gene Plaisted, OSC : 193 *top.*
Myrleen Cate : 22, 28, 32–33, 34, 38–39, 39 *top,* 57, 69, 72, 75, 84, 88, 89, 108, 125, 128, 134, 139 *bottom right,* 140, 154 *bottom,* 158–159, 160, 169, 175, 178, 182 *bottom right,* 183, 184, 194 *top,* 193 *bottom left.*
Lochon/ Liaison : 109 *left.*
H. Armstrong Roberts : 25, 137, 139 *top.*
Nancy Sheehan : 8–9, 10, 114–115, 115, 120, 146, 147,154 *center,* 194 bottom *left.*
Vernon Sigl : 146–147.
Howard E. Simmons : 121, 154 *top,* 182 *top.*

Illustrators

Blaine Martin : Cover, Digital Imaging
Wendy Pierson : Cover, Logo Rendering
Angela Adams : 78, 148B, 160.
Marilyn Barr : 16, 57, 60, 107, 119, 131, 145, 148A.
Andrea Barrett : 181, 193.
David Barrett : 44–45.
Shirley Beckes : 96, 158–159.
Kevin Butler : 11, 12, 17.
Janice Castiglione : 31.
Antonio Castro : 64, 65.
Gwen Connelly : 88–89.
Eulala Conner : 93, 102–103, 154, 166, 170.
Doug Cushman : 129, 167, 173.
Renee Daily : 126–127.
Len Ebert : 35, 195.
Allan Eitzen : 14–15.
Collin Fry : 161.
Kate Gorman : 135.
Ronda Hendrichsen : 104, 172, 175, 178.
Sharon Holm : 41, 47, 141.
Roberta Holmes : 111.
Sunshine De La Rosa Jouvin : 40.
Laura Kelly : 76–77, 122.
Anne Kennedy : 189.
Eliot Kreloff : 116.
Cecily Lang : 53, 97, 117.
Susan Lexa : 7, 26–27, 46, 52, 66, 151.
Dora Leder : 19, 49.
Anita Lovitt : 23, 67, 79.
Diana Magnuson : 13, 43, 50–51, 63, 81, 94–95.
Ben Mahan : 105.
Anni Matsick : 20–21, 37, 101.
Jim McConnell : 85.
Jane C. Morgan : 22.
Carol Nicklaus : 194, sticker art.
Kathleen O'Malley : 155.
Lainé Roundy : 8, 9, 138–139.
Mark Samuels : 61, 91.
Margaret Sanfilippo : 58–59, 164–165, 176–177.
Tom Sperling : 132–133, 152–153.
Gerardo Suzan : 73.
Peggy Tagel : 108–109, 123, 149.
Marina Thompson : 29.
Stan Tusan : 125, 169, 171.
David Wenzel : 70–71.
Jenny Williams : 87, 90, 110 157, 163.

200

OUR CATHOLIC IDENTITY

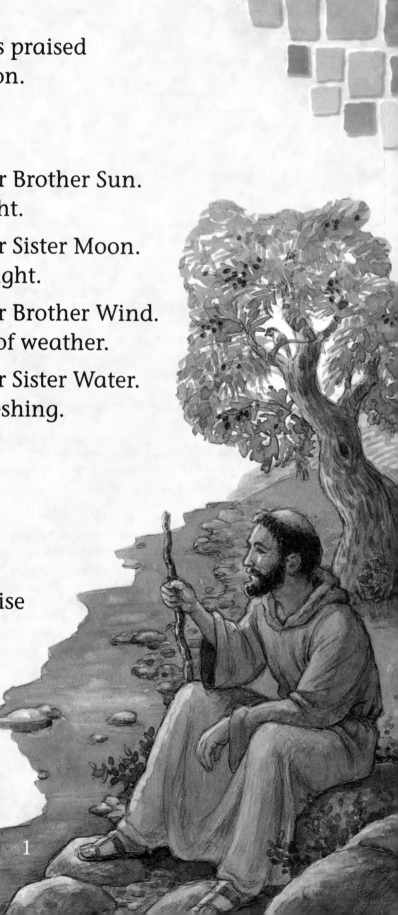

Praising God's Creation

Saint Francis loved everything in God's creation.

This is the way Saint Francis praised and thanked God for creation.

✝Be praised, O God, for Brother Sun.
  He gives us your light.

Be praised, O God, for Sister Moon.
  She brightens the night.

Be praised, O God, for Brother Wind.
  He brings all kinds of weather.

Be praised, O God, for Sister Water.
  She is cool and refreshing.

Add your own prayer to praise God for something you love in the world.

Learn by heart **Faith Summary**

- God made everything.

- All God's creation is good.

1

Making the Sign of the Cross

Catholics make the sign of the cross when we begin and end our prayers.

We make the sign of the cross with holy water when we go into church.

When the priest blesses us at the end of Mass, we make the sign of the cross again.

Every time we make the sign of the cross, we should think of what we are saying.

Let's make the sign of the cross together now.

Learn by heart Faith Summary

- God knows and loves us.

- God made us to love one another.

Good Listeners

God speaks to us in many ways.
God wants us to be listeners—really
good listeners.
How can you be a good listener?

One way is to be very still,
very quiet with God.
God will be with you.

You can be very still, too, at Mass
when God's stories are read.
You can pay attention to the stories.
You can tell them to others.

You can be a good listener in your
religion class.
Listen as your teacher tells you
about God.
Listen to what your friends say
about God, too.

What kind of a listener will you be
this year?

 Learn by heart **Faith Summary**

- People turned away from God.

- God promised to save us and
  gave us Jesus, God's own Son.

3

The Foster Father of Jesus

Jesus had a foster father.
He was Jesus' special protector.
We call him Saint Joseph.

Even before Jesus was born, Joseph loved and took care of Mary. Then Joseph loved Jesus and cared for Him. Joseph taught Jesus how to be a carpenter. He also helped Jesus to pray and read the Bible.

Think about someone who loves and protects you.

Draw pictures of some of the things these people do for you.

Ask Saint Joseph to care for those who protect you.

Learn by heart **Faith Summary**

- Jesus is God's own Son.
- Jesus is one of us.

4

The Name of Jesus

The name of Jesus is very holy.
We use it only with respect.
Catholics often bow their heads
when they hear or say His name.
We do this to show love and
respect for the holy name of Jesus.

Here is a prayer to Jesus.
Pray it together.
When you say Jesus' name,
bow your head.

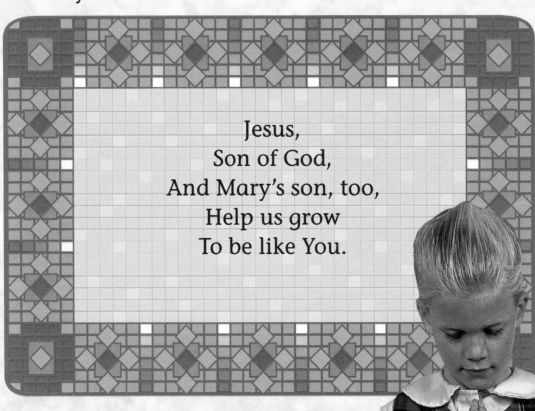

Jesus,
Son of God,
And Mary's son, too,
Help us grow
To be like You.

Learn by heart **Faith Summary**

- Jesus is God's greatest gift
  to us.

- Jesus shows us He is
  God's own Son.

5

Praying for Others

Do you know that you can help other people by your prayers? We can ask God to comfort or heal someone.

Praying for others is like giving them a special gift.

God always hears our prayers for others. God answers them in a way that is best for each person.

Work together to make cards for people in your parish who need your prayers. Pray together for each person by name.

Learn by heart **Faith Summary**

- Jesus cares for all people.

- We can pray to Jesus our friend.

Praying Hands

Some people pray with their hands folded. Others have their hands outstretched. Still others hold hands. Can you tell other ways we can use our bodies to pray to God?

Tell about the different ways and times you like to pray. Draw a picture that shows one of the ways and times you like to pray.

It could be your morning and evening prayers, your mealtime prayers, prayers at Mass, or when you are alone.

Learn by heart **Faith Summary**

- God is like a loving parent.

- Jesus taught us the Law of Love.

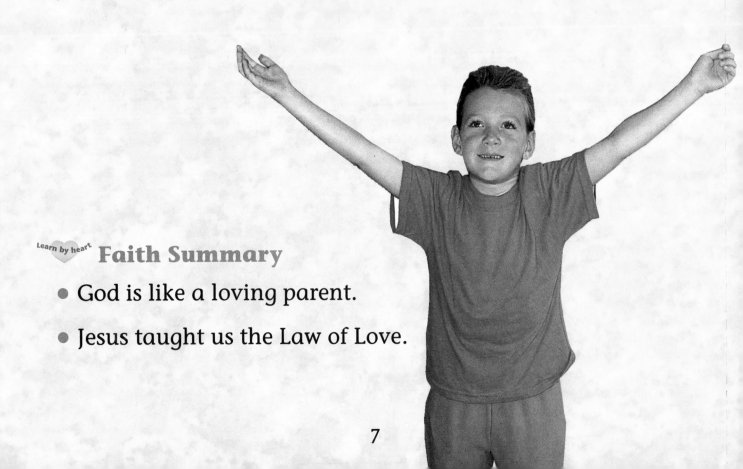

7

Church

Tell what comes to your mind when you hear the word Church. Maybe you thought of a building with a cross. Maybe you thought of going to Mass. Did you ever think of people?

The Church is not just a building or a celebration. It is all the baptized people who believe in God and in Jesus Christ, the Son of God.

This means we are the Church. The Church is the people of God. All over the world the people of God believe and worship and care for others.

Tell how you are part of the Church.

Learn by heart Faith Summary

- Jesus invites everyone to belong to His Church.

- We are part of the Church and try to treat others as Jesus did.

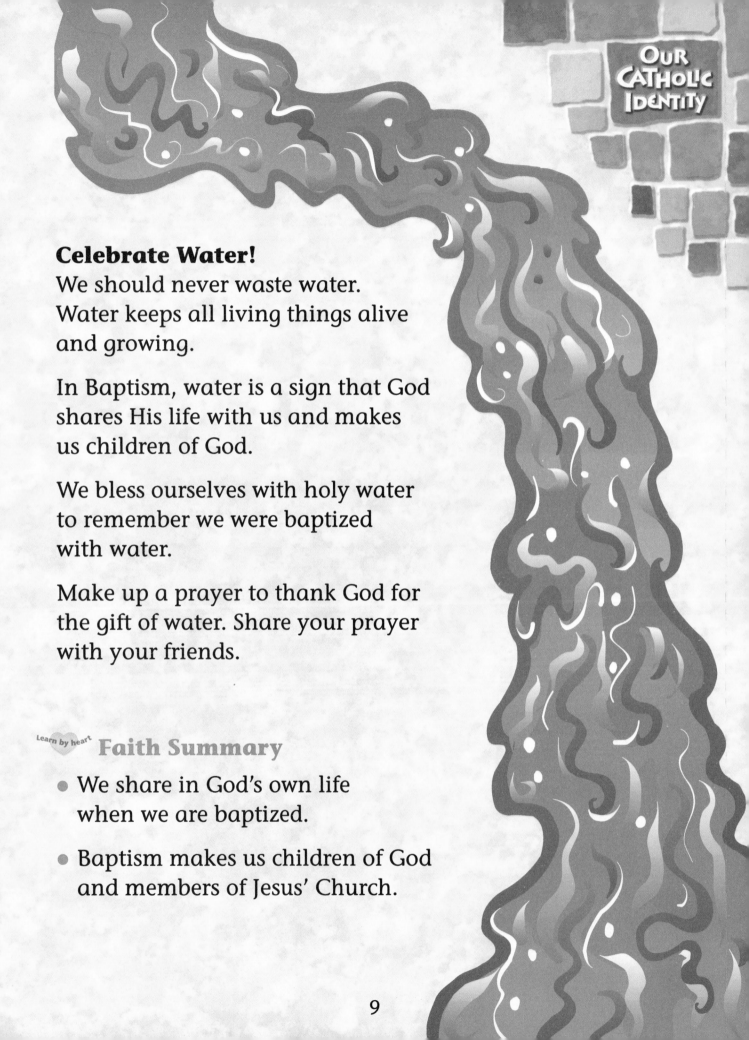

Celebrate Water!

We should never waste water. Water keeps all living things alive and growing.

In Baptism, water is a sign that God shares His life with us and makes us children of God.

We bless ourselves with holy water to remember we were baptized with water.

Make up a prayer to thank God for the gift of water. Share your prayer with your friends.

Learn by heart
Faith Summary

- We share in God's own life when we are baptized.

- Baptism makes us children of God and members of Jesus' Church.

Our Greeting at Mass

Friends have special ways to greet each other. Some friends kiss or hug. Others shake hands and say, "I'm glad to see you."

Share your special way to greet your friends.

The friends of Jesus greet one another at Mass. The priest opens his arms wide to welcome us. He may say, "The Lord be with you." We answer together, "And also with you."

This greeting reminds us that we are a family of Jesus' friends. Jesus is with us at Mass. We are happy to celebrate together.

The next time you go to Mass, listen for the special greeting, "The Lord be with you." What will you answer?

Learn by heart Faith Summary

- Jesus is with us each time we celebrate the Mass.

- We all have a part to play in the Mass.

Amen, Amen, Amen!

Amen is a wonderful prayer.
When we pray Amen we tell God,
"Yes, I believe!"

We say Amen at the end of every
prayer we learn. We also say
Amen many times at Mass.
When Communion time comes,
the priest or eucharistic minister
holds up the Host and says,
"The Body of Christ." Those who
receive answer, "Amen."

Our Amen means that we believe
Jesus is with us in Holy Communion.

Make up an Amen prayer.
Tell Jesus something you
believe about Him.

> †Jesus, I believe
>
> _____
>
> --
>
> _____ Amen!

Take turns praying your prayer.

Learn by heart **Faith Summary**
- We listen to God's word at Mass.
- Our gifts to God become Jesus, whom
  we receive in Holy Communion.

A Visit to Our Parish Church

Our parish church belongs to all of us. It is filled with things that remind us of God's love for us.

Look at the pictures of things we see in our parish church. What does each one tell us about God's love for us?

Ask someone in your family to take you to church for a visit. Talk about the things you see. Say a prayer together to thank God for loving you so much.

Learn by heart **Faith Summary**

- Our parish is our special place in the Catholic Church.

- Everyone helps in our parish.

12

Sharing Peace

During Mass we can show that we want to be peacemakers, too.

Just before we receive Jesus in Holy Communion, we share a sign of peace with those around us.

Let us share a sign of peace now. Shake hands with one another and say, "The peace of Christ be with you."

Color the banner and then say this prayer for peacemakers.

✝ Let Jesus' peace be with me.

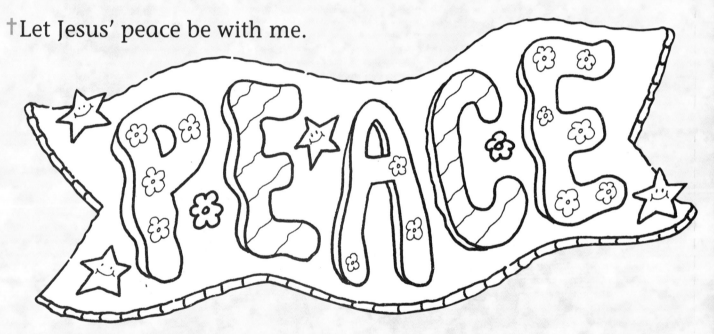

Learn by heart **Faith Summary**

● Catholics try to treat others fairly and live in peace.

● Jesus wants us to be peacemakers.

We Think About Our Day

How do you know if you are growing as a child of God? Catholics have a special way to think about this.

Find a quiet place to think about the things you did today.

- Did you pray to God?
- Did you play fair?
- Did you forgive someone?
- Did you obey the people who take care of you?
- Did you take care of yourself by eating good food?
- Were you kind to someone in need?

Thank God for the good things you did today. Tell God you are sorry for the things you may have done that are wrong. Ask God to help you find ways to do better tomorrow.

Learn by heart  Faith Summary

- God always forgives us if we are sorry.

- The priest forgives us in God's name.

14

Praise Our Loving God

The Church has a beautiful prayer to praise and honor the Blessed Trinity.

In this prayer, we praise God, who is Father, Son, and Holy Spirit.

Gather in a friendship circle.

Let us end our year together by praising God. We can repeat this prayer until all of us know it well.

✝ Glory to the Father,
and to the Son,
and to the Holy Spirit
as it was in the beginning,
is now, and will be
for ever. Amen.

Learn by heart Faith Summary

- Jesus wants us to be with Him forever.

- God's love will never end.